From Ritual to Romance

Other works by Jessie Laidlay Weston (1850–1928):

Legends of the Wagner Drama (1896)
The Legend of Sir Gawain (1897)
King Arthur and His Knights (1899)
The Romance of Charlemagne and His Peers (1900)
The Legend of Sir Lancelot du Lac (1901)
The Three Days' Tournament (1902)
Sir Gawain and the Green Knight (1905)
Sir Gawain and the Lady of Lys (1907)
The Legend of Sir Percival vol. i (1906), vol. ii (1909)
A Hitherto Unconsidered Aspect of the Round Table (1910)
Romance, Vision and Satire English Alliterative Poems of the 14th century (1912)
The Quest of the Holy Grail (1913)
(Editor) *The Chief Middle English Poets* (1914)
Germany's Literary Debt to France (1915)
From Ritual to Romance (1920) (Awarded the Crawshay Prize for 1920)

JESSIE L. WESTON

From Ritual to Romance

DOUBLEDAY ANCHOR BOOKS
DOUBLEDAY & COMPANY, INC.
GARDEN CITY, NEW YORK

Cover by Leonard Baskin
Typography by Edward Gorey

From Ritual to Romance was originally published by
Cambridge University Press in 1920. The Anchor Books
edition is published by arrangement with Cambridge
University Press.

Anchor Books edition: 1957

*For this edition the citations of verse
and prose excerpts have been
translated by Mary M. McLaughlin*

"Animus ad amplitudinem Mysteri-
orum pro modulo suo dilatetur, non
Mysteria ad angustias animi constring-
antur." Bacon

"Many literary critics seem to think
that an hypothesis about obscure and
remote questions of history can be re-
futed by a simple demand for the pro-
duction of more evidence than in fact
exists.—But the true test of an hypothesis,
if it cannot be shewn to conflict with
known truths, is the number of facts that
it correlates, and explains." (Cornford,
Origins of Attic Comedy)

Preface

In the introductory Chapter the reader will find the aim and object of these studies set forth at length. In view of the importance and complexity of the problems involved it seemed better to incorporate such a statement in the book itself, rather than relegate it to a Preface which all might not trouble to read. Yet I feel that such a general statement does not adequately express my full debt of obligation.

Among the many whose labour has been laid under contribution in the following pages there are certain scholars whose published work, or personal advice, has been specially illuminating, and to whom specific acknowledgment is therefore due. Like many others I owe to Sir J. G. Frazer the initial inspiration which set me, as I may truly say, on the road to the Grail castle. Without the guidance of *The Golden Bough* I should probably, as the late M. Gaston Paris happily expressed it, still be wandering in the forest of Broceliande!

During the Bayreuth Festival of 1911 I had frequent opportunities of meeting, and discussion with, Professor von Schroeder. I owe to him not only the introduction to his own work, which I found most helpful, but references which have been of the greatest assistance; *e.g.* my knowledge of Cumont's *Les Religions Orientales*, and Scheftelowitz's valuable study on *Fish Symbolism*, both of which have furnished important links in the chain of evidence, is due to Professor von Schroeder.

The perusal of Miss J. E. Harrison's *Themis* opened my eyes to the extended importance of these Vegetation rites. In view of the evidence there adduced I asked myself whether beliefs which had found expression not only in social institution, and popular custom, but, as set forth in Sir G. Murray's study on Greek Dramatic Origins, attached to the work, also in Drama and Literature, might not reasonably—even inevitably—be expected to have left their mark on Romance? The one seemed to me a necessary corollary of the other, and I felt that I had gained, as the result of Miss Harrison's work, a wider, and more assured basis for my own researches. I was no longer engaged merely in enquiring into the sources of a fascinating legend, but on the identification of another field of activity for forces whose potency as agents of evolution we were only now beginning rightly to appreciate.

Finally, a casual reference, in Anrich's work on the Mysteries, to the *Naassene Document*, caused me to apply to Mr G. R. S. Mead, of whose knowledge of the mysterious border-land between Christianity and Paganism, and willingness to place that knowledge at the disposal of others, I had, for some years past, had pleasant experience. Mr Mead referred me to his own translation and analysis of the text in question, and there, to my satisfaction, I found, not only the final link that completed the chain of evolution from Pagan Mystery to Christian Ceremonial, but also proof of that wider significance I was beginning to apprehend. The problem involved was not one of Folk-lore, not even one of Literature, but of Comparative Religion in its widest sense.

Thus, while I trust that my co-workers in the field of Arthurian research will accept these studies as a permanent contribution to the elucidation of the Grail problem, I would fain hope that those scholars who labour in a wider field, and to whose works I owe so much, may find in the results here set forth elements that may prove of real value in the study of the evolution of religious belief.

J. L. W.

Paris,
October, 1919.

Contents

CHAPTER I

Introductory

Nature of the Grail problem. Unsatisfactory character of results achieved. Objections to Christian Legendary origin; to Folk-lore origin. Elements in both theories sound. Solution to be sought in a direction which will do justice to both. Sir J. G. Frazer's *Golden Bough* indicates possible line of research. Sir W. Ridgeway's criticism of *Vegetation* theory examined. *Dramas and Dramatic Dances.* The Living and not the Dead King the factor of importance. Impossibility of proving human origin for Vegetation Deities. Not Death but Resurrection the essential centre of Ritual. *Muharram* too late in date and lacks Resurrection feature. Relation between defunct heroes and special localities. Sanctity possibly antecedent to connection. *Mana* not necessarily a case of relics. Self-acting weapons frequent in Medieval Romance. Sir J. G. Frazer's theory holds good. Remarks on method and design of present Studies.

CHAPTER II

The Task of the Hero

Essential to determine the original nature of the task imposed upon the hero. Versions examined. The GAWAIN forms—*Bleheris, Diû Crône.* PERCEVAL versions—*Gerbert, prose Perceval, Chrétien de Troyes, Perlesvaus, Manessier, Peredur, Parzival.* GALAHAD—*Queste.* Result, primary task healing of Fisher King and removal of curse of Waste Land. The two inter-dependent. Illness of King entails misfortune on Land. Enquiry into nature of King's disability. *Sone de Nansai.* For elucidation of problem necessary to bear in mind close connection between Land and Ruler. Importance of Waste Land *motif* for criticism.

CHAPTER V

Medieval and Modern Forms of Nature Ritual

Is it possible to establish chain of descent connecting early Aryan and Babylonian Ritual with Classic, Medieval and Modern forms of Nature worship? Survival of Adonis cult established. Evidence of Mannhardt and Frazer. Existing Continental customs recognized as survivals of ancient beliefs. Instances. 'Directly related' to Attis-Adonis cult. Von Schroeder establishes parallel between existing Fertility procession and *Rig-Veda* poem. Identification of Life Principle with King. Prosperity of land dependent on king as representative of god. Celts. Greeks. Modern instances, the Shilluk Kings. Parallel between Shilluk King, Grail King and Vegetation Deity. *Sone de Nansai* and the *Lament for Tammuz*. Identity of situation. Plea for unprejudiced criticism. Impossibility of such parallels being fortuitous; the result of deliberate intention, not an accident of literary invention. If identity of central character be admitted his relation to Waste Land becomes fundamental factor in criticizing versions. Another African survival.

CHAPTER VI

The Symbols

Summary of results of previous enquiry. *The Mediaeval Stage.* Grail romances probably contain record of secret ritual of a Fertility cult. The Symbols of the cult—Cup, Lance, Sword, Stone, or Dish. Plea for treating Symbols as a related group not as isolated units. Failure to do so probably cause of unsatisfactory result of long research. Essential to recognize Grail story as an original whole and to treat it in its *ensemble* aspect. We must differentiate between origin and accretion. Instances. *The Legend of Longinus.* Lance and Cup not associated in Christian Art. Evidence. The *Spear* of Eastern Liturgies only a *Knife. The Bleeding Lance.* Treasures of the Tuatha de Danann. Correspond as a group with Grail Symbols. Difficulty of equating Cauldron-Grail. Probably belong to a different line of tradition. Instances given. Real significance of Lance and Cup. Well known as Life Symbols. The Samurai. Four Symbols also preserved as

CHAPTER XI

The Secret of the Grail
(2) The Naassene Document

CHAPTER XII

Mithra and Attis

CHAPTER XIII

The Perilous Chapel

CHAPTER XIV

The Author

CHAPTER I

Introductory

In view of the extensive literature to which the Grail legend has already given birth it may seem that the addition of another volume to the already existing *corpus* calls for some words of apology and explanation. When the student of the subject contemplates the countless essays and brochures, the volumes of studies and criticism, which have been devoted to this fascinating subject, the conflicting character of their aims, their hopelessly contradictory results, he, or she, may well hesitate before adding another element to such a veritable witches' cauldron of apparently profitless study. And indeed, were I not convinced that the theory advocated in the following pages contains in itself the element that will resolve these conflicting ingredients into one harmonious compound I should hardly feel justified in offering a further contribution to the subject.

But it is precisely because upwards of thirty years' steady and persevering study of the Grail texts has brought me gradually and inevitably to certain very definite conclusions, has placed me in possession of evidence hitherto ignored, or unsuspected, that I venture to offer the result in these studies, trusting that they may be accepted as, what I believe them to be, a genuine *Elucidation* of the Grail problem.

My fellow-workers in this field know all too well the essential elements of that problem; I do not need here to go over already well-trodden ground; it will be sufficient to point out certain salient features of the position.

The main difficulty of our research lies in the fact that the Grail legend consists of a congeries of widely differing elements—elements which at first sight appear hopelessly incongruous, if not completely contradictory, yet at the same time are present to an extent, and in a form, which no honest critic can afford to ignore.

Thus it has been perfectly possible for one group of scholars, relying upon the undeniably Christian-Legendary elements, preponderant in certain versions, to maintain the thesis that the Grail legend is *ab initio* a Christian, and ecclesiastical, legend, and to analyse the literature on that basis alone.

Another group, with equal reason, have pointed to the strongly marked Folk-lore features preserved in the tale, to its kinship with other themes, mainly of Celtic *provenance,* and have argued that, while the later versions of the cycle have been worked over by ecclesiastical writers in the interests of edification, the story itself is non-Christian, and Folk-lore in origin.

Both groups have a basis of truth for their arguments: the features upon which they rely are, in each case, undeniably present, yet at the same time each line of argument is faced with certain insuperable difficulties, fatal to the claims advanced.

Thus, the theory of Christian origin breaks down when faced with the awkward fact that there is no Christian legend concerning Joseph of Arimathea and the Grail. Neither in Legendary, nor in Art, is there any trace of the story; it has no existence outside the Grail literature, it is the creation of romance, and no genuine tradition.

On this very ground it was severely critized by the Dutch writer Jacob van Maerlant, in 1260. In his

Merlin he denounces the whole Grail history as lies, asserting that the Church knows nothing of it—which is true.

In the same way the advocate of a Folk-lore origin is met with the objection that that section of the cycle for which such a source can be definitely proved, *i.e.*, the *Perceval* story, has originally nothing whatever to do with the Grail; and that, while parallels can be found for this or that feature of the legend, such parallels are isolated in character and involve the breaking up of the tale into a composite of mutually independent themes. A prototype, containing the main features of the Grail story—the Waste Land, the Fisher King, the Hidden Castle with its solemn Feast, and mysterious Feeding Vessel, the Bleeding Lance and Cup—does not, so far as we know, exist. None of the great collections of Folk-tales, due to the industry of a Cosquin, a Hartland, or a Campbell, has preserved specimens of such a type; it is not such a story as, *e.g.*, *The Three Days Tournament*, examples of which are found all over the world. Yet neither the advocate of a Christian origin, nor the Folk-lorist, can afford to ignore the arguments, and evidence of the opposing school, and while the result of half a century of patient investigation has been to show that the origin of the Grail story must be sought elsewhere than in ecclesiastical legend, or popular tale, I hold that the result has equally been to demonstrate that neither of these solutions should be ignored, but that the ultimate source must be sought for in a direction which shall do justice to what is sound in the claims of both.

Some years ago, when fresh from the study of Sir J. G. Frazer's epoch-making work, *The Golden Bough*, I was struck by the resemblance existing between certain features of the Grail story, and characteristic details of the Nature Cults described. The more closely I analysed the tale, the more striking became the resemblance, and I finally asked myself whether it were not possible that in this mysterious legend—mysterious alike in its character, its sudden appearance, the importance apparently assigned to it, followed by as sudden and complete a disappearance—we might not have the confused record of a ritual, once popular, later surviving under conditions of strict secrecy? This would fully account for the atmosphere of awe and reverence which even under distinctly non-Christian conditions never fails to surround the Grail, It may act simply as a feeding vessel, It is none the less *toute sainte cose;* and also for the presence in the tale of distinctly popular, and Folk-lore, elements. Such an interpretation would also explain features irreconcilable with orthodox Christianity, which had caused some scholars to postulate a heterodox origin for the legend, and thus explain its curiously complete disappearance as a literary theme. In the first volume of my *Perceval* studies, published in 1906, I hinted at this possible solution of the problem, a solution worked out more fully in a paper read before the Folk-lore Society in December of the same year, and published in Volume xviii. of the Journal of the Society. By the time my second volume of studies was ready for publication in 1909, further evidence had come into my hands; I was then certain that I was upon the right path, and I felt justified in laying before the public the outlines of a theory of evolution, alike of the legend, and of the literature, to the main principles of which I adhere to-day.

But certain links were missing in the chain of evidence, and the work was not complete. No inconsiderable part of the information at my disposal depended upon personal testimony, the testimony of those who knew of the continued existence of such a ritual, and had actually been initiated into its mysteries—and for such evidence the student of the letter has little respect. He worships the written word; for the oral, living, tradition from which the word derives force and vitality he has little use. Therefore the written word had to be found. It has taken me some nine or ten years longer to complete the evidence, but the chain is at last linked up, and we can now prove by printed texts the parallels existing between each and every feature of the Grail story and the recorded symbolism of the Mystery cults. Further, we can show that between these Mystery cults and Christianity there existed at one time a close and intimate union, such a union as of itself involved the practical assimilation of the central rite, in each case a 'Eucharistic' Feast, in which the worshippers partook of the Food of Life from the sacred vessels.

In face of the proofs which will be found in these pages I do not think any fair-minded critic will be inclined to dispute any longer the origin of the 'Holy' Grail; after all it is as august and ancient an origin as the most tenacious upholder of Its Christian character could desire.

But I should wish it clearly to be understood that the aim of these studies is, as indicated in the title, to determine the *origin* of the Grail, not to discuss the *provenance* and interrelation of the different versions. I do not believe this latter task can be satisfactorily achieved unless and until we are of one accord as to the character of the subject matter. When we have made up our minds as to what the Grail really was, and what it stood for, we shall be able to analyse the romances; to decide which of them contains more, which less, of the original matter, and to group them accordingly. On this point I believe that the table of descent, printed in Volume

II. of my *Perceval* studies is in the main correct, but there is still much analytical work to be done, in particular the establishment of the original form of the *Perlesvaus* is highly desirable. But apart from the primary object of these studies, and the results therein obtained, I would draw attention to the manner in which the evidence set forth in the chapters on the Mystery cults, and especially that on *The Naassene Document*, a text of extraordinary value from more than one point of view, supports and complements the researches of Sir J. G. Frazer. I am, of course, familiar with the attacks directed against the 'Vegetation' theory, the sarcasms of which it has been the object, and the criticisms of what is held in some quarters to be the exaggerated importance attached to these Nature cults. But in view of the use made of these cults as the medium of imparting high spiritual teaching, a use which, in face of the document above referred to, can no longer be ignored or evaded, are we not rather justified in asking if the true importance of the rites has as yet been recognized? Can we possibly exaggerate their value as a factor in the evolution of religious consciousness?

Such a development of his researches naturally lay outside the range of Sir J. G. Frazer's work, but posterity will probably decide that, like many another patient and honest worker, he 'builded better than he knew.'

I have carefully read Sir W. Ridgeway's attack on the school in his *Dramas and Dramatic Dances*, and while the above remarks explain my position with regard to the question as a whole, I would here take the opportunity of stating specifically my grounds for dissenting from certain of the conclusions at which the learned author arrives. I do not wish it to be said: "This is all very well, but Miss Weston ignores the arguments on the other side." I do not ignore, but I do not admit their validity. It is perfectly obvious that Sir W. Ridgeway's theory, reduced to abstract terms, would result in the conclusion that all religion is based upon the cult of the Dead, and that men originally knew no gods but their grandfathers, a theory from which as a student of religion I absolutely and entirely dissent. I can understand that such Dead Ancestors can be looked upon as Protectors, or as Benefactors, but I see no ground for supposing that they have ever been regarded as Creators, yet it is precisely as vehicle for the most lofty teaching as to the Cosmic relations existing between God and Man, that these Vegetation cults were employed. The more closely one studies pre-Christian Theology, the more strongly one is impressed with the deeply, and daringly, spiritual character of its speculations, and the more doubtful it appears that such teaching can depend upon the unaided processes of human thought, or can have been evolved from such germs as we find among the supposedly 'primitive' peoples, such as *e.g.*, the Australian tribes. Are they really primitive? Or are we dealing, not with the primary elements of religion, but with the *disjecta membra* of a vanished civilization? Certain it is that so far as historical evidence goes our earliest records point to the recognition of a spiritual, not of a material, origin of the human race; the Sumerian and Babylonian Psalms were not composed by men who believed themselves the descendants of 'witchetty grubs.' The Folk practices and ceremonies studied in these pages, the Dances, the rough Dramas, the local and seasonal celebrations, do not represent the material out of which the Attis-Adonis cult was formed, but surviving fragments of a worship from which the higher significance has vanished.

Sir W. Ridgeway is confident that Osiris, Attis,

Adonis, were all at one time human beings, whose tragic fate gripped hold of popular imagination, and led to their ultimate deification. The first-named cult stands on a somewhat different basis from the others, the beneficent activities of Osiris being more widely diffused, more universal in their operation. I should be inclined to regard the Egyptian deity primarily as a Culture Hero, rather than a Vegetation God.

With regard to Attis and Adonis, whatever their original character (and it seems to me highly improbable that there should have been two youths each beloved by a goddess, each victim of a similar untimely fate), long before we have any trace of them both have become so intimately identified with the processes of Nature that they have ceased to be men and become gods, and as such alone can we deal with them. It is also permissible to point out that in the case of Tammuz, Esmun, and Adonis, the title is not a proper name, but a vague appellative, denoting an abstract rather than a concrete origin. Proof of this will be found later. Sir W. Ridgeway overlooks the fact that it is not the tragic death of Attis-Adonis which is of importance for these cults, but their subsequent restoration to life, a feature which cannot be postulated of any ordinary mortal.

And how are we to regard Tammuz, the prototype of all these deities? Is there any possible ground for maintaining that he was ever a man? Prove it we cannot, as the records of his cult go back thousands of years before our era. Here, again, we have the same dominant feature; it is not merely the untimely death which is lamented, but the restoration to life which is celebrated.

Throughout the whole study the author fails to discriminate between the activities of the living, and the dead, king. The Dead king may, as I have said above, be regarded as the Benefactor, as the Protector, of his people, but it is the Living king upon whom their actual and continued prosperity depends. The detail that the ruling sovereign is sometimes regarded as the re-incarnation of the original founder of the race strengthens this point—the king never dies—*Le Roi est mort, Vive le Roi* is very emphatically the motto of this Faith. It is the insistence on Life, Life continuous, and ever-renewing, which is the abiding characteristic of these cults, a characteristic which differentiates them utterly and entirely from the ancestral worship with which Sir W. Ridgeway would fain connect them.

Nor are the arguments based upon the memorial rites of definitely historical heroes, of comparatively late date, such as Hussein and Hossein, of any value here. It is precisely the death, and not the resurrection, of the martyr which is of the essence of the Muharram. No one contends that Hussein rose from the dead, but it is precisely this point which is of primary importance in the Nature cults; and Sir W. Ridgeway must surely be aware that Folk-lorists find in this very Muharram distinct traces of borrowing from the earlier Vegetation rites.

The author triumphantly asserts that the fact that certain Burmese heroes and heroines are after death reverenced as tree spirits 'sets at rest for ever' the belief in abstract deities. But how can he be sure that the process was not the reverse of that which he postulates, *i.e.*, that certain natural objects, trees, rivers, etc., were not regarded as sacred *before* the Nats became connected with them? That the deified human beings were not after death assigned to places already held in reverence? Such a possibility is obvious to any Folk-lore student, and local traditions should in each case be carefully examined before the contrary is definitely asserted.

So far as the origins of Drama are concerned the

Ode quoted later from the Naassene Document is absolute and definite proof of the close connection existing between the Attis Mystery ritual, and dramatic performances, *i.e.*, Attis regarded in his deified, Creative, 'Logos,' aspect, not Attis, the dead youth.

Nor do I think that the idea of 'Mana' can be lightly dismissed as 'an ordinary case of relics.' The influence may well be something entirely apart from the continued existence of the ancestor, an independent force, assisting him in life, and transferring itself after death to his successor. A 'Magic' Sword or Staff is not necessarily a relic; Medieval romance supplies numerous instances of self-acting weapons whose virtue in no wise depends upon their previous owner, as *e.g.*, the Sword in *Le Chevalier à l'Épée*, or the Flaming Lance of the *Chevalier de la Charrette*. Doubtless the cult of Ancestors plays a large *rôle* in the beliefs of certain peoples, but it is not a sufficiently solid foundation to bear the weight of the super-structure Sir W. Ridgeway would fain rear upon it, while it differs too radically from the cults he attacks to be used as an argument against them; the one is based upon Death, the other on Life.

Wherefore, in spite of all the learning and ingenuity brought to bear against it, I avow myself an impenitent believer in Sir J. G. Frazer's main theory, and as I have said above, I hold that theory to be of greater and more far-reaching importance than has been hitherto suspected.

I would add a few words as to the form of these studies—they may be found disconnected. They have been written at intervals of time extending over several years, and my aim has been to prove the essentially archaic character of *all* the elements composing the Grail story rather than to analyse the story as a connected whole. With this aim in view I have devoted chapters to features which have now either dropped out of the existing versions, or only survive in a subordinate form, *e.g.*, the chapters on *The Medicine Man,* and *The Freeing of the Waters.* The studies will, I hope, and believe, be accepted as offering a definite contribution towards establishing the fundamental character of our material; as stated above, when we are all at one as to what the Holy Grail really was, and is, we can then proceed with some hope of success to criticize the manner in which different writers have handled the inspiring theme, but such success seems to be hopeless so long as we all start from different, and often utterly irreconcilable, standpoints and proceed along widely diverging roads. One or another may, indeed, arrive at the goal, but such unanimity of opinion as will lend to our criticism authoritative weight is, on such lines, impossible of achievement.

CHAPTER II

The Task of the Hero

As a first step towards the successful prosecution of an investigation into the true nature and character of the mysterious object we know as the Grail it will be well to ask ourselves whether any light may be thrown upon the subject by examining more closely the details of the Quest in its varying forms; *i.e.*, what was the precise character of the task undertaken by, or imposed upon, the Grail hero, whether that hero were Gawain, Perceval, or Galahad, and what the results to be expected from a successful achievement of the task. We shall find at once a uniformity which assures us of the essential identity of the tradition underlying the varying forms, and a diversity indicating that that tradition has undergone a gradual, but radical, modification in the process of literary evolution. Taken in their relative order the versions give the following result.

GAWAIN (*Bleheris*). Here the hero sets out on his journey with no clear idea of the task before him. He is taking the place of a knight mysteriously slain in his company, but whither he rides, and why, he does not know, only that the business is important and pressing. From the records of his partial success we gather that he ought to have enquired concerning the nature of the Grail, and that this enquiry would have resulted in the restoration to fruitfulness of a Waste Land, the desolation of which is, in some manner, not clearly explained, connected with

the death of a knight whose name and identity are
never disclosed. "Great is the loss that ye lie thus,
'tis even the destruction of kingdoms, God grant that
ye be avenged, so that the folk be once more joyful
and the land repeopled which by ye and this sword
are wasted and made void."[1] The fact that Gawain
does ask concerning the Lance assures the partial
restoration of the land; I would draw attention to
the special terms in which this is described: "for so
soon as Sir Gawain asked of the Lance . . . the
waters flowed again thro' their channel, and all the
woods were turned to verdure."[2]

Diû Crône. Here the question is more general in
character; it affects the marvels beheld, not the Grail
alone; but now the Quester is prepared, and knows
what is expected of him. The result is to break the
spell which retains the Grail King in a semblance of
life, and we learn, by implication, that the land is
restored to fruitfulness: "yet had the land been
waste, but by his coming had folk and land alike
been delivered."[3] Thus in the earliest preserved,
the GAWAIN, form, the effect upon the land appears
to be the primary result of the Quest.

PERCEVAL. The *Perceval* versions, which form the
bulk of the existing Grail texts, differ considerably
the one from the other, alike in the task to be
achieved, and the effects resulting from the hero's
success, or failure. The distinctive feature of the
Perceval version is the insistence upon the sickness,
and disability of the ruler of the land, the Fisher
King. Regarded first as the direct cause of the wasting of the land, it gradually assumes overwhelming
importance, the task of the Quester becomes that of

[1] MS. Bibl. Nat., f. Franç. 12576, fo. 90.
[2] *Ibid.* fo. 90vo, 91.
[3] *Diû Crône* (ed. Stoll, Stuttgart, 1852). Cf. *Sir Gawain at the Grail Castle* for both versions.

healing the King, the restoration of the land not
only falls into the background but the operating
cause of its desolation is changed, and finally it
disappears from the story altogether. One version,
alone, the source of which is, at present, undetermined, links the PERCEVAL with the GAWAIN form;
this is the version preserved in the Gerbert continuation of the *Perceval* of Chrétien de Troyes. Here the
hero having, like Gawain, partially achieved the
task, but again like Gawain, having failed satisfactorily to resolder the broken sword, wakes, like the
earlier hero, to find that the Grail castle has disappeared, and he is alone in a flowery meadow. He
pursues his way through a land fertile, and well-
peopled and marvels much, for the day before it
had been a waste desert. Coming to a castle he is
received by a solemn procession, with great rejoicing; through him the folk have regained the land and
goods which they had lost. The mistress of the
castle is more explicit. Perceval had asked concerning the Grail:

> "All this was done by what he said,
>   This land whose streams no waters fed,
>   Its fountains dry, its fields unplowed,
>   His word once more with health endowed."

Like Gawain he has 'freed the waters' and thus
restored the land.[4]

In the prose *Perceval* the *motif* of the Waste Land
has disappeared, the task of the hero consists in
asking concerning the Grail, and by so doing, to
restore the Fisher King, who is suffering from extreme old age, to health, and youth.[5]

"If you had asked what was happening, your

[4] Cf. MS. B.N. 12576, fo. 154.
[5] *Perceval*, ed. Hucher, p. 466; Modena, p. 61.

question would have cured the king's infirmity and he would have been restored to youth."

When the question has been asked: "The Fisher King was cured and his condition wholly changed." "The Fisher King's condition was changed, and he was cured of his malady, and was as healthy as a fish."[6] Here we have the introduction of a new element, the restoration to youth of the sick King.

In the *Perceval* of Chrétien de Troyes we find ourselves in presence of certain definite changes, neither slight, nor unimportant, upon which it seems to me insufficient stress has hitherto been laid. The question is changed; the hero no longer asks what the Grail is, but (as in the prose *Perceval*) whom it serves? a departure from an essential and primitive simplicity—the motive for which is apparent in Chrétien, but not in the prose form, where there is no enigmatic personality to be served apart. A far more important change is that, while the malady of the Fisher King is antecedent to the hero's visit, and capable of cure if the question be asked, the failure to fulfil the prescribed conditions of itself entails disaster upon the land. Thus the sickness of the King, and the desolation of the land, are not necessarily connected as cause and effect, but, a point which seems hitherto unaccountably to have been overlooked, the latter is directly attributable to the Quester himself.[7]

> "If you had found the word to say,
> The rich king who in distress does lay
> Would of his wound be fully healed.
> But now his fate is truly sealed,
> Never to rule his land in peace,"

[6] Cf. Hucher, p. 482; Modena, p. 82.
[7] *Perceval li Gallois*, ed. Potvin, ll. 6048–52.

but by Perceval's failure to ask the question he has
entailed dire misfortune upon the land:

> "Ladies sad will lose their mates,
>   The land in desolation lie,
>   Damsels unconsoled will sigh,
>   Widows and orphans, mournful all,
>   And many a knight in death will fall."[8]

This idea, that the misfortunes of the land are not
antecedent to, but dependent upon, the hero's
abortive visit to the Grail castle, is carried still
further by the compiler of the *Perlesvaus*, where
the failure of the predestined hero to ask concerning
the office of the Grail is alone responsible for the
illness of the King and the misfortunes of the
country. "A great sorrow has recently been brought
on the land by a young knight who was welcomed
as a guest by the rich Fisher King. To him appeared
the Holy Grail and the lance with angry blood
welling from its point. He did not ask whom it
served or whence it came, and because he did not
ask this, all the lands are stirred up to war and no
knight meets another in the forest without striking
him down and killing him if he can."[9]

"The Fisher King is very sorrowful, for he has
fallen into a doleful sickness. This sickness has come
upon him through one whom he welcomed as a
guest, to whom the Holy Grail appeared, and because he did not ask whom it served, all the lands
were stirred up to war."[10]

"I have fallen into languishment from the hour
when the knight of whom you have heard tell was
harboured as a guest here. Because of one word that

[8] *Ib.* ll. 6056–60.
[9] Potvin, Vol. I. p. 15.
[10] *Ib.* p. 26.

he delayed to speak, this languishment came upon me."[11]

From this cause the Fisher King dies before the hero has achieved the task, and can take his place. "The good Fisher King is dead."[12] There is here no cure of the King or restoration of the land, the specific task of the Grail hero is never accomplished, he comes into his kingdom as the result of a number of knightly adventures, neither more nor less significant than those found in non-Grail romances.

The *Perlesvaus*, in its present form, appears to be a later, and more fully developed, treatment of the *motif* noted in Chrétien, *i.e.*, that the misfortunes of King and country are directly due to the Quester himself, and had no antecedent existence; this, I would submit, alters the whole character of the story, and we are at a loss to know what, had the hero put the question on the occasion of his first visit, could possibly have been the result achieved. It would not have been the cure of the King: he was, apparently, in perfect health; it would not have been the restoration to verdure of the Land: the Land was not Waste; where, as in the case of Gawain, there is a Dead Knight, whose death is to be avenged, *something* might have been achieved, in the case of the overwhelming majority of the *Perceval* versions, which do not contain this feature, the dependence of the Curse upon the Quester reduces the story to incoherence. In one *Perceval* version alone do we find a *motif* analogous to the earlier *Gawain Bleheris* form. In Manessier the hero's task is not restricted to the simple asking of a question, but he must also slay the enemy whose treachery has caused the death of the Fisher King's brother; thereby healing the wound of the King

11 *Ib*. p. 86.
12 *Ib*. pp. 176, 178.

himself, and removing the woes of the land. What these may be we are not told, but, apparently, the country is not 'Waste.'[13]

In *Peredur* we have a version closely agreeing with that of Chrétien; the hero fails to enquire the meaning of what he sees in the Castle of Wonders, and is told in consequence: "Hadst thou done so the King would have been restored to health, and his dominions to peace, whereas from henceforth he will have to endure battles and conflicts, and his knights will perish, and wives will be widowed, and maidens will be left portionless, and all this because of thee."[14] This certainly seems to imply that, while the illness of the Fisher King may be antecedent to, and independent of, the visit and failure of the hero, the misfortunes which fall on the land have been directly caused thereby.

The conclusion which states that the Bleeding Head seen by the hero "was thy cousin's, and he was killed by the Sorceresses of Gloucester, who also lamed thine uncle—and there is a prediction that thou art to avenge these things—" would seem to indicate the presence in the original of a 'Vengeance' theme, such as that referred to above.[15]

In *Parzival* the stress is laid entirely on the sufferings of the King; the question has been modified in the interests of this theme, and here assumes the form "What aileth thee, mine uncle?" The blame bestowed upon the hero is solely on account of the prolonged sorrow his silence has inflicted on King and people; of a Land laid Waste, either through drought, or war, there is no mention.

> "You should have pitied the host and king
> To whom God did this wondrous thing.

[13] MS. B.N. 12576, ff. 221–222vo.
[14] *Mabinogion*, ed. Nutt, p. 282.
[15] Cf. *Peredur* (ed. Nutt), pp. 282, 291–92.

You asked not of his grief and dread,
So though you live, your bliss is dead."[16]

"When unconsoled the Fisher sat,
So sorrowful and full of grief,
Why would you not give him relief?"[17]

The punishment falls on the hero who has failed
to put the question, rather than on the land, which,
indeed, appears to be in no way affected, either by
the wound of the King, or the silence of the hero.
The divergence from Chrétien's version is here very
marked, and, so far, seems to have been neglected
by critics. The point is also of importance in view
of the curious parallels which are otherwise to be
found between this version and *Perlesvaus;* here
the two are in marked contradiction with one
another.

The question finally asked, the result is, as indicated in the prose version, the restoration of the
King not merely to health, but also to youth—

"Over his skin there spread a blush,
'Flori' the Frenchmen call this flush.
His face at once became so fair,
It made Parzival's beauty vain as air,
And that of Absalom, David's son,
And Vergulaht of Ascalun.
All who from birth in beauty grew,
Like Gahmuret, as men well knew,
When into Kanvoleis he went,
His glory seeming heaven-sent,
All these in no way could compare
With King Anfortas' beauty rare
When cured and freed of all his ills,
He proved that God has wondrous skills."[18]

16 *Parzival*, Book v. ll. 947–50.
17 *Ib.* Book vi. ll. 1078–80.
18 *Parzival*, Book xvi. ll. 275–86.

GALAHAD. In the final form assumed by the story, that preserved in the *Queste*, the achievement of the task is not preceded by any failure on the part of the hero, and the advantages derived therefrom are personal and spiritual, though we are incidentally told that he heals the Fisher King's father, and also the old King, Mordrains, whose life has been preternaturally prolonged. In the case of this latter it is to be noted that the mere fact of Galahad's being the predestined winner suffices, and the healing takes place *before* the Quest is definitely achieved.

There is no Waste Land, and the wounding of the two Kings is entirely unconnected with Galahad. We find hints, in the story of Lambar, of a knowledge of the earlier form, but for all practical purposes it has disappeared from the story.[19]

Analysing the above statements we find that the results may be grouped under certain definite headings:

(*a*) There is a general consensus of evidence to the effect that the main object of the Quest is the restoration to health and vigour of a King suffering from infirmity caused by wounds, sickness, or old age;

(*b*) and whose infirmity, for some mysterious and unexplained reason, reacts disastrously upon his kingdom, either depriving it of vegetation, or exposing it to the ravages of war.

(*c*) In two cases it is definitely stated that the King will be restored to youthful vigour and beauty.

(*d*) In both cases where we find Gawain as the hero of the story, and in one connected with Perceval, the misfortune which has fallen upon the country is that of a prolonged drought, which has destroyed

---

[19] Cf. *Morte Arthure*, Malory, Book XVII. Chap. 18. Note the remark of Mordrains that his flesh which has waxen old shall become young again.

vegetation, and left the land Waste; the effect of the hero's question is to restore the waters to their channel, and render the land once more fertile.

(*e*) In three cases the misfortunes and wasting of the land are the result of war, and directly caused by the hero's failure to ask the question; we are not dealing with an antecedent condition. This, in my opinion, constitutes a marked difference between the two groups, which has not hitherto received the attention it deserves. One aim of our present investigation will be to determine which of these two forms should be considered the elder.

But this much seems certain, the aim of the Grail Quest is two-fold; it is to benefit (*a*) the King, (*b*) the land. The first of these two is the more important, as it is the infirmity of the King which entails misfortune on his land, the condition of the one reacts, for good or ill, upon the other; how, or why, we are left to discover for ourselves.

Before proceeding further in our investigation it may be well to determine the precise nature of the King's illness, and see whether any light upon the problem can be thus obtained.

In both the *Gawain* forms the person upon whom the fertility of the land depends is dead, though, in the version of *Diû Crône* he is, to all appearance, still in life. It should be noted that in the *Bleheris* form the king of the castle, who is not referred to as the Fisher King, is himself hale and sound; the wasting of the land was brought about by the blow which slew the knight whose body Gawain sees on the bier.

In both the *Perlesvaus*, and the prose *Perceval* the King has simply 'fallen into languishment,' in the first instance, as noted above, on account of the failure of the Quester, in the second as the result of extreme old age.

In Chrétien, Manessier, *Peredur,* and the *Parzival,* the King is suffering from a wound the nature of which, euphemistically disguised in the French texts, is quite clearly explained in the German.[20]

But the whole position is made absolutely clear by a passage preserved in *Sone de Nansai* and obviously taken over from an earlier poem. This romance contains a lengthy section dealing with the history of Joseph 'd'Abarimathie,' who is represented as the patron Saint of the kingdom of Norway; his bones, with the sacred relics of which he had the charge, the Grail and the Lance, are preserved in a monastery on an island in the interior of that country. In this version Joseph himself is the Fisher King; ensnared by the beauty of the daughter of the Pagan King of Norway, whom he has slain, he baptizes her, though she is still an unbeliever at heart, and makes her his wife, thus drawing the wrath of Heaven upon himself. God punishes him for his sin:

> "His loins are stricken by this bane
> From which he suffers lasting pain."[21]

Then, in a remarkable passage, we are told of the direful result entailed by this punishment upon his land:

> "Lorgres his land was from this day
> Called by all, and truth to say,
> Well should Lorgres be named with tears,
> With bitter weeping, grief and fears.
> For here no fertile seed is sown,
> Neither peas nor grain are grown,
> Never a child of man is born,
> Mateless maidens sadly mourn,

[20] *Parzival,* Bk. IX. ll. 1388–92.
[21] *Sone de Nansai* (ed. Goldschmidt, Stuttgart, 1899), ll. 4775–76.

On the trees no leaf is seen
Nor are the meadows growing green,
Birds build no nests, no song is sung,
And hapless beasts shall bear no young,
So is it while the sinful king
Shall evil on his people bring.
For Jesus Christ does punish well
The land wherein the wicked dwell."[22]

Now there can be no possible doubt here, the condition of the King is sympathetically reflected on the land, the loss of virility in the one brings about a suspension of the reproductive processes of Nature on the other. The same effect would naturally be the result of the death of the sovereign upon whose vitality these processes depended.

To sum up the result of the analysis, I hold that we have solid grounds for the belief that the story postulates a close connection between the vitality of a certain King, and the prosperity of his kingdom; the forces of the ruler being weakened or destroyed, by wound, sickness, old age, or death, the land becomes Waste, and the task of the hero is that of restoration.[23]

It seems to me, then, that, if we desire to elucidate the perplexing mystery of the Grail romances, and to place the criticism of this important and singularly fascinating body of literature upon an assured basis, we shall do so most effectually by pursuing a line of investigation which will concentrate upon the persistent elements of the story, the character and significance of the achievement proposed, rather

[22] *Sone de Nansai*, ll. 4841–56.
[23] It is evidently such a version as that of *Sone de Nansai*, and *Parzival*, which underlies the curious statement of the *Merlin* MS. B.N., f. Fr. 337, where the wife of the Fisher King is known as 'la Veve Dame,' while her husband is yet in life, though sorely wounded.

than upon the varying details, such as Grail and
Lance, however important may be their *rôle*. If we
can ascertain, accurately, and unmistakably, the
meaning of the whole, we shall, I think, find less
difficulty in determining the character and office
of the parts, in fact, the question *solvitur ambulando*,
the 'complex' of the problem being solved, the con-
stituent elements will reveal their significance.

As a first step I propose to ask whether this 'Quest
of the Grail' represents an isolated, and unique
achievement, or whether the task allotted to the
hero, Gawain, Perceval, or Galahad, is one that has
been undertaken, and carried out by heroes of other
ages, and other lands. In the process of our investigation we must retrace our steps and turn back to
the early traditions of our Aryan forefathers, and
see whether we cannot, even in that remote antiquity, lay our hand upon a clue, which, like the fabled
thread of Ariadne, shall serve as guide through the
mazes of a varying, yet curiously persistent, tradition.

CHAPTER III

The Freeing of the Waters

'To begin at the beginning,' was the old story-telling formula, and it was a very sound one, if 'the beginning' could only be definitely ascertained! As our nearest possible approach to it I would draw attention to certain curious parallels in the earliest literary monuments of our race. I would at the same time beg those scholars who may think it 'a far cry' from the romances of the twelfth century of our era to some 1000 years B.C. to suspend their judgment till they have fairly examined the evidence for a tradition common to the Aryan race in general, and persisting with extraordinary vitality, and a marked correspondence of characteristic detail, through all migrations and modifications of that race, down to the present day.

Turning back to the earliest existing literary evidence, the *Rig-Veda,* we become aware that, in this vast collection of over 1000 poems (it is commonly known as *The Thousand and One Hymns* but the poems contained in it are more than that in number) are certain parallels with our Grail stories which, if taken by themselves, are perhaps interesting and suggestive rather than in any way conclusive, yet which, when they are considered in relation to the entire body of evidence, assume a curious significance and importance. We must first note that a very considerable number of the *Rig-Veda* hymns depend for their initial inspiration on the actual bodily needs and requirements of a mainly agricultural population, *i.e.*, of a people that depend upon the fruits of the earth for their subsistence, and to whom the regular and ordered sequence of the processes of Nature was a vital necessity.

Their hymns and prayers, and, as we have strong reason to suppose, their dramatic ritual, were devised for the main purpose of obtaining from the gods of their worship that which was essential to ensure their well-being and the fertility of their land—warmth, sunshine, above all, sufficient water. That this last should, in an Eastern land, under a tropical sun, become a point of supreme importance, is easily to be understood. There is consequently small cause for surprise when we find, throughout the collection, the god who bestows upon them this much desired boon to be the one to whom by far the greater proportion of the hymns are addressed. It is not necessary here to enter into a discussion as to the original conception of Indra, and the place occupied by him in the early Aryan Pantheon, whether he was originally regarded as a god of war, or a god of weather; what is important for our purpose is the fact that it is Indra to whom a disproportionate number of the hymns of the *Rig-Veda* are addressed, that it is from him the much desired boon of rain and abundant water is besought, and that the feat which above all others redounded to his praise, and is ceaselessly glorified both by the god himself, and his grateful worshippers, is precisely the feat by which the Grail heroes, Gawain and Perceval, rejoiced the hearts of a suffering folk, *i.e.*, the restoration of the rivers to their channels, the 'Freeing of the Waters.' Tradition relates that the seven great rivers of India had been imprisoned by the evil giant, Vṛitra, or Ahi, whom Indra slew, thereby releasing the streams from their captivity.

The *Rig-Veda* hymns abound in references to this feat; it will only be necessary to cite a few from among the numerous passages I have noted.

'Thou hast set loose the seven rivers to flow.'

'Thou causest water to flow on every side.'

'Indra set free the waters.'

'Thou, Indra, hast slain Vritra by thy vigour, thou hast set free the rivers.'

'Thou hast slain the slumbering Ahi for the release of the waters, and hast marked out the channels of the all-delighting rivers.'

'Indra has filled the rivers, he has inundated the dry land.'

'Indra has released the imprisoned waters to flow upon the earth.'[1]

It would be easy to fill pages with similar quotations, but these are sufficient for our purpose.

Among the *Rig-Veda* hymns are certain poems in Dialogue form, which from their curious and elliptic character have been the subject of much discussion among scholars. Professor Oldenberg, in drawing attention to their peculiarities, had expressed his opinion that these poems were the remains of a distinct type of early Indian literature, where verses forming the central, and illuminating, point of a formal ceremonial recital had been 'farced' with illustrative and explanatory prose passages; the form of the verses being fixed, that of the prose being varied at the will of the reciter.[2]

This theory, which is technically known as the 'Âkhyâna' theory (as it derived its starting point from the discussion of the Suparnâkhyâna text), won

[1] Cf. *Rig-Veda Sanhita*, trans. H. H. Wilson, 6 vols. 1854–1888. Vol. I. p. 88, v. 12. 172, v. 8. 206, v. 10. Vol. III. p. 157, vv. 2, 5, 7, 8.

[2] *Zeitschrift der Deutschen Morgenlandischen Geschichte*, Vols. XXXVII. and XXXIX.

considerable support, but was contested by M. Sylvain Lévi, who asserted that, in these hymns, we had the remains of the earliest, and oldest, Indian dramatic creations, the beginning of the Indian Drama; and that the fragments could only be satisfactorily interpreted from the point of view that they were intended to be spoken, not by a solitary reciter, but by two or more *dramatis personae*.[3]

J. Hertel (*Der Ursprung des Indischen Dramas und Epos*) went still further, and while accepting, and demonstrating, the justice of this interpretation of the 'Dialogue' poems, suggested a similar origin for certain 'Monologues' found in the same collection.[4]

Professor Leopold von Schroeder, in his extremely interesting volume, *Mysterium und Mimus im Rig-Veda*,[5] has given a popular and practical form to the results of these researches, by translating and publishing, with an explanatory study, a selection of these early 'Culture' Dramas, explaining the speeches, and placing them in the mouth of the respective actors to whom they were, presumably, assigned. Professor von Schroeder holds the entire group to be linked together by one common intention, *viz.*, the purpose of stimulating the processes of Nature, and of obtaining, as a result of what may be called a Ritual Culture Drama, an abundant return of the fruits of the earth. The whole book is rich in parallels drawn from ancient and modern sources, and is of extraordinary interest to the Folk-lore student.

In the light thrown by Professor von Schroeder's

[3] Cf. *Le Théâtre Indien*, Paris, 1890.

[4] Cf. *Wiener Zeitsch. für die Kunde des Morgenlandes*, Vol. XVIII. 1904.

[5] Leipzig, 1908.

researches, following as they do upon the illuminating studies of Mannhardt, and Frazer, we become strikingly aware of the curious vitality and persistence of certain popular customs and beliefs; and while the two last-named writers have rendered inestimable service to the study of Comparative Religion by linking the practices of Classical and Medieval times with the Folk-customs of to-day, we recognize, through von Schroeder's work, that the root of such belief and custom is imbedded in a deeper stratum of Folk-tradition than we had hitherto realized, that it is, in fact, a heritage from the far-off past of the Aryan peoples.

For the purposes of our especial line of research *Mysterium und Mimus* offers much of value and interest. As noted above, the main object of these primitive Dramas was that of encouraging, we may say, ensuring, the fertility of the Earth; thus it is not surprising that more than one deals with the theme of which we are treating, the Freeing of the Waters, only that whereas, in the quotations given above, the worshippers praise Indra for his beneficent action, here Indra himself, in *propria persona* appears, and vaunts his feat.

"I struck down Vṛitra by the power of Indra!
 I had become so strong in fury!
 For all mankind I set the rivers free."[6]

And the impersonated rivers speak for themselves.

"Indra armed with the thunderbolt broke the way
     for us,
He smote down Vṛitra, the encloser of the rivers."[7]

There is no need to insist further on the point that the task of the Grail hero is in this special respect

[6] *Op. cit.* p. 105.
[7] *Ib.* p. 230.

no mere literary invention, but a heritage from the achievements of the prehistoric heroes of the Aryan race.

But the poems selected by Professor von Schroeder for discussion offer us a further, and more curious, parallel with the Grail romances.

In Section VIII. of the work referred to the author discusses the story of Ṛishyaçriṅga, as the *Mahâbhârata* names the hero; here we find a young Brahmin brought up by his father, Vibhândaka, in a lonely forest hermitage[8] absolutely ignorant of the outside world, and even of the very existence of beings other than his father and himself. He has never seen a woman, and does not know that such a creature exists.

A drought falls upon a neighbouring kingdom, and the inhabitants are reduced to great straits for lack of food. The King, seeking to know by what means the sufferings of his people may be relieved, learns that so long as Ṛishyaçriṅga continues chaste so long will the drought endure. An old woman, who has a fair daughter of irregular life, undertakes the seduction of the hero. The King has a ship, or raft (both versions are given), fitted out with all possible luxury, and an apparent Hermit's cell erected upon it. The old woman, her daughter and companions, embark; and the river carries them to a point not far from the young Brahmin's hermitage.

Taking advantage of the absence of his father, the girl visits Ṛishyaçriṅga in his forest cell, giving him to understand that she is a Hermit, like himself, which the boy, in his innocence, believes. He is so fascinated by her appearance and caresses that, on her leaving him, he, deep in thought of the lovely visitor, forgets, for the first time, his religious duties.

[8] *Ib.* p. 292, for sources, and variants of tale.

On his father's return he innocently relates what has happened, and the father warns him that fiends in this fair disguise strive to tempt hermits to their undoing. The next time the father is absent the temptress, watching her opportunity, returns, and persuades the boy to accompany her to her 'Hermitage' which she assures him, is far more beautiful than his own. So soon as Rishyaçriṅga is safely on board the ship sails, the lad is carried to the capital of the rainless land, the King gives him his daughter as wife, and so soon as the marriage is consummated the spell is broken, and rain falls in abundance.

Professor von Schroeder points out that there is little doubt that, in certain earlier versions of the tale, the King's daughter herself played the *rôle* of temptress.

There is no doubt that a ceremonial 'marriage' very frequently formed a part of 'Fertility' ritual, and was supposed to be specially efficacious in bringing about the effect desired.[9] The practice subsists in Indian ritual to this hour, and the surviving traces in European Folk-custom have been noted in full by Mannhardt in his exhaustive work on *Wald und Feld-Kulte;* its existence in Classic times is well known, and it is certainly one of the living Folk-customs for which a well-attested chain of descent can be cited. Professor von Schroeder remarks that the efficacy of the rite appears to be enhanced by the previous strict observance of the rule of chastity by the officiant.[10]

What, however, is of more immediate interest for our purpose is the fact that the Rishyaçriṅga

[9] On this point cf. Cornford, *Origin of Attic Comedy,* pp. 8, 78, for importance of this feature.

[10] *Op. cit.* pp. 161–170, for general discussion of question, and summary of authorities. Also pp. 297 *et seq.*

story does, in effect, possess certain curious points of contact with the Grail tradition.

Thus, the lonely upbringing of the youth in a forest, far from the haunts of men, his absolute ignorance of the existence of human beings other than his parent and himself, present a close parallel to the accounts of Perceval's youth and woodland life, as related in the Grail romances.[11]

In Gerbert's continuation we are told that the marriage of the hero is an indispensable condition of achieving the Quest, a detail which must have been taken over from an earlier version, as Gerbert proceeds to stultify himself by describing the solemnities of the marriage, and the ceremonial blessing of the nuptial couch, after which hero and heroine simultaneously agree to live a life of strict chastity, and are rewarded by the promise that the Swan Knight shall be their descendant—a tissue of contradictions which can only be explained by the *mal-à-droit* blending of two versions, one of which knew the hero as wedded, the other, as celibate. There can be no doubt that the original *Perceval* story included the marriage of the hero.[12]

The circumstances under which Ṛishyaçṛiṅga is lured from his Hermitage are curiously paralleled by the account, found in the *Queste* and Manessier, of Perceval's temptation by a fiend, in the form of a fair maiden, who comes to him by water in a vessel hung with black silk, and with great riches on board.[13]

In pointing out these parallels I wish to make my position perfectly clear; I do not claim that either in the *Rig-Veda*, or in any other early Aryan literary monument, we can hope to discover the direct

[11] Cf. *Legend of Sir Perceval*, Vol. I. Chapter 3.

[12] MS. Bibl. Nat., f. Fr. 12576, fo. 173. Cf. also *Legend of Sir Perceval*, I. Chap. 4.

[13] Malory, *Morte Arthure*, Book XIV. Chaps. 8 and 9. Potvin, ll. 40420 *et seq.*

sources of the Grail legend, but what I would urge upon scholars is the fact that, in adopting the hypothesis of a Nature Cult as a possible origin, and examining the history of these Cults, their evolution, and their variant forms, we do, in effect, find at every period and stage of development undoubted points of contact, which, though taken separately, might be regarded as accidental, in their *ensemble* can hardly be thus considered. When every parallel to our Grail story is found within the circle of a well-defined, and carefully studied, sequence of belief and practice, when each and all form part of a well-recognized body of tradition the descent of which has been abundantly demonstrated, then I submit such parallels stand on a sound basis, and it is not unreasonable to conclude that the body of tradition containing them belongs to the same family and is to be interpreted on the same principles as the closely analogous rites and ceremonies.

I suspend the notice and discussion of other poems contained in Prof. von Schroeder's collection till we have reached a later stage of the tradition, when their correspondence will be recognized as even more striking and suggestive.

CHAPTER IV

Tammuz and Adonis

PART I.   TAMMUZ

IN the previous chapter we considered certain aspects of the attitude assumed by our Aryan forefathers towards the great processes of Nature in their ordered sequence of Birth, Growth, and Decay. We saw that while on one hand they, by prayer and supplication, threw themselves upon the mercy of the Divinity, who, in their belief, was responsible for the granting, or withholding, of the water, whether of rain, or river, the constant supply of which was an essential condition of such ordered sequence, they, on the other hand, believed that, by their own actions, they could stimulate and assist the Divine activity. Hence the dramatic representations to which I have referred, the performance, for instance, of such a drama as the Ṛishyaçṛiṅga, the ceremonial 'marriages,' and other exercises of what we now call sympathetic magic. To quote a well-known passage from Sir J. G. Frazer: "They commonly believed that the tie between the animal and vegetable world was even closer than it really is—to them the principle of life and fertility, whether animal or vegetable, was one and indivisible. Hence actions that induced fertility in the animal world were held to be equally efficacious in stimulating the reproductive energies of the vegetable."[1] How deeply this idea was rooted in the minds of our

[1] Cf. Frazer, *Adonis, Attis, Osiris*, p. 5.

ancestors we, their descendants, may learn from its survival to our own day.

The ultimate, and what we may in a general sense term the classical, form in which this sense of the community of the Life principle found expression was that which endowed the vivifying force of Nature with a distinct personality, divine, or semi-divine, whose experiences, in virtue of his close kinship with humanity, might be expressed in terms of ordinary life.

At this stage the progress of the seasons, the birth of vegetation in spring, or its revival after the autumn rains, its glorious fruition in early summer, its decline and death under the maleficent influence either of the scorching sun, or the bitter winter cold, symbolically represented the corresponding stages in the life of this anthropomorphically conceived Being, whose annual progress from birth to death, from death to a renewed life, was celebrated with a solemn ritual of corresponding alternations of rejoicing and lamentation.

Recent research has provided us with abundant material for the study of the varying forms of this Nature Cult, the extraordinary importance of which as an evolutionary factor in what we may term the concrete expression of human thought and feeling is only gradually becoming realized.[2]

Before turning our attention to this, the most important, section of our investigation, it may be well to consider one characteristic difference between the

---

[2] In this connection not only the epoch-making works of Mannhardt and Frazer, which are more specifically devoted to an examination of Folk-belief and practice should be studied, but also works such as *The Mediaeval Stage*, E. K. Chambers; *Themis*, J. E. Harrison; *The Origin of Attic Comedy*, F. Cornford; and Sir Gilbert Murray's essay on the evolution of the Greek Drama, published in Miss Harrison's *Themis*. The cumulative evidence of these works is most striking.

Nature ritual of the *Rig-Veda*, and that preserved to us in the later monuments of Greek antiquity.

In the *Rig-Veda*, early as it is, we find the process of religious evolution already far advanced; the god has separated himself from his worshippers, and assumed an anthropomorphic form. Indra, while still retaining traces of his 'weather' origin, is no longer, to borrow Miss Harrison's descriptive phrase, 'an automatic explosive thunder-storm,' he wields the thunderbolt certainly, but he appears in heroic form to receive the offerings made to him, and to celebrate his victory in a solemn ritual dance. In Greek art and literature, on the other hand, where we might expect to find an even more advanced conception, we are faced with one seemingly more primitive and inchoate, *i.e.*, the idea of a constantly recurring cycle of Birth, Death, and Resurrection, or Re-Birth, of all things in Nature, this cycle depending upon the activities of an entity at first vaguely conceived of as the 'Luck of the Year,' the *Eniautos Daimon*. This Being, at one stage of evolution theriomorphic—he might assume the form of a bull, a goat, or a snake (the latter, probably from the close connection of the reptile with the earth, being the more general form) —only gradually, and by distinctly traceable stages, assumed an anthropomorphic shape.[3] This gives to the study of Greek antiquity a special and peculiar value, since in regard to the body of religious belief and observance with which we are here immediately concerned, neither in what we may not improperly term its ultimate (early Aryan), nor in what has been generally considered its proximate (Syro-Phoenician), source, have these intermediate stages been preserved; in each case the ritual remains are illus-

---

[3] A full study of this evolutionary process will be found in Miss Harrison's *Themis, A Study in Greek Social Origins,* referred to above.

trative of a highly developed cult, distinctly anthropomorphic in conception. I offer no opinion as to the
critical significance of this fact, but I would draw the
attention of scholars to its existence.

That the process of evolution was complete at a
very early date has been proved by recent researches
into the Sumerian-Babylonian civilization. We know
now that the cult of the god Tammuz, who, if not the
direct original of the Phoenician-Greek Adonis, is at
least representative of a common parent deity, may
be traced back to 3000 B.C., while it persisted among
the Sabeans at Harran into the Middle Ages.[4]

While much relating to the god and his precise
position in the Sumerian-Babylonian Pantheon still
remains obscure, fragmentary cuneiform texts connected with the religious services of the period have
been discovered, and to a considerable extent deciphered, and we are thus in a position to judge, from
the prayers and invocations addressed to the deity,
what were the powers attributed to, and the benefits
besought from, him. These texts are of a uniform
character; they are all 'Lamentations,' or 'Wailings,'
having for their exciting cause the disappearance of
Tammuz from this upper earth, and the disastrous
effects produced upon animal and vegetable life by
his absence. The woes of the land and the folk are
set forth in poignant detail, and Tammuz is passion-
ately invoked to have pity upon his worshippers, and
to end their sufferings by a speedy return. This return, we find from other texts, was effected by the
action of a goddess, the mother, sister, or paramour,

[4] Baudissin, in his exhaustive study of these cults, *Adonis
und Esmun*, comes to the conclusion that Tammuz and Adonis
are different gods, owing their origin to a common parent
deity. Where the original conception arose is doubtful;
whether in Babylon, in Canaan, or in a land where the common ancestors of Phoenicians and Babylonian Semites formed
an original unit.

of Tammuz, who, descending into the nether world, induced the youthful deity to return with her to earth. It is perfectly clear from the texts which have been deciphered that Tammuz is not to be regarded merely as representing the Spirit of Vegetation; his influence is operative, not only in the vernal processes of Nature, as a Spring god, but in all its reproductive energies, without distinction or limitation, he may be considered as an embodiment of the Life principle, and his cult as a Life Cult.

Mr Stephen Langdon inclines to believe that the original Tammuz typified the vivifying waters; he writes: "Since, in Babylonia as in Egypt, the fertility of the soil depended upon irrigation, it is but natural to expect that the youthful god who represents the birth and death of nature, would represent the beneficent waters which flooded the valleys of the Tigris and Euphrates in the late winter, and which ebbed away, and nearly disappeared, in the canals and rivers in the period of Summer drought. We find therefore that the theologians regarded this youthful divinity as belonging to the cult of Eridu, centre of the worship of Ea, lord of the nether sea."[5] In a note to this passage Mr Langdon adds: "He appears in the great theological list as *Dami-zi, ab-zu,* 'Tammuz of the nether sea,' *i.e.,* 'the faithful son of the fresh waters which come from the earth.'"[6]

---

[5] Cf. *Tammuz and Ishtar,* S. Langdon, p. 5.

[6] It may be well to note here that the 'Life' deity has no proper name; he is only known by an appellative; *Damu-zi, Damu,* 'faithful son,' or 'son and consort,' is only a general epithet, which designates the dying god in a theological aspect, just as the name *Adōni,* 'my lord,' certainly replaced a more specific name for the god of Byblos. *Esmun* of Sidon, another type of Adonis, is a title only, and means simply, 'the name.' Cf. Langdon, *op. cit.* p. 7. Cf. this with previous passages on the evolution of the Greek idea from a nameless entity to a definite god. Mr Langdon's remarks on the evolution of the Tammuz cult should be carefully studied in view

This presents us with an interesting analogy to the citations given in the previous chapter from the *Rig-Veda;* the Tammuz cult is specially valuable as providing us with evidence of the gradual evolution of the Life Cult from the early conception of the vivifying power of the waters, to the wider recognition of a common principle underlying all manifestations of Life.

This is very clearly brought out in the beautiful Lament for Tammuz, published by Mr Langdon in *Tammuz and Ishtar,* and also in *Sumerian and Babylonian Psalms.*[7]

"In Eanna, high and low, there is weeping,
Wailing for the house of the lord they raise.
The wailing is for the plants; the first lament is 'they grow not.'
The wailing is for the barley; the ears grow not.
For the habitations and flocks it is; they produce not.
For the perishing wedded ones, for perishing children it is; the dark-headed people create not.
The wailing is for the great river; it brings the flood no more.
The wailing is for the fields of men; the gunū grows no more.
The wailing is for the fish-ponds; the dasuḫur fish spawn not.
The wailing is for the cane-brake; the fallen stalks grow not.
The wailing is for the forests; the tamarisks grow not.
The wailing is for the highlands; the masgam trees grow not.

---

of the theory maintained by Sir W. Ridgeway—that the Vegetation deities were all of them originally men.

[7] From a liturgy employed at Nippur in the period of the Isin dynasty. Langdon, *op. cit.* p. 11. Also, *Sumerian and Babylonian Psalms,* p. 338.

The wailing is for the garden store-house; honey and
  wine are produced not.
The wailing is for the meadows; the bounty of the
  garden, the siḫtū plants grow not.
The wailing is for the palace; life unto distant days
  is not."

Can anything be more expressive of the community of life animating the whole of Nature than this
poignantly worded lament?

A point which differentiates the worship of Tammuz from the kindred, and better known, cult of
Adonis, is the fact that we have no liturgical record
of the celebration of the resurrection of the deity; it
certainly took place, for the effects are referred to:

"Where grass was not, there grass is eaten,
  Where water was not, water is drunk,
  Where the cattle sheds were not, cattle sheds are
    built."[8]

While this distinctly implies the revival of vegetable and animal life, those features (*i.e.*, resurrection and sacred marriage), which made the Adonis
ritual one of rejoicing as much as of lamentation, are
absent from liturgical remains of the Tammuz cult.[9]

A detail which has attracted the attention of scholars is the lack of any artistic representation of this
ritual, a lack which is the more striking in view of the
important position which these 'Wailings for Tammuz' occupy in the extant remains of Babylonian

[8] Cf. Langdon, *Tammuz and Ishtar*, p. 23.
[9] What we have been able to ascertain of the Sumerian-
Babylonian religion points to it rather as a religion of mourning and supplication, than of joy and thanksgiving. The people seem to have been in perpetual dread of their gods, who
require to be appeased by continual acts of humiliation. Thus
the 9th, 15th, 19th, 28th, and 29th of the month were all days
of sack-cloth and ashes, days of wailing; the 19th especially
was 'the day of the wrath of Gulu.'

liturgies. On this point Mr Langdon makes an interesting suggestion: "It is probable that the service of wailing for the dying god, the descent of the mother, and the resurrection, were attended by mysterious rituals. The actual mysteries may have been performed in a secret chamber, and consequently the scenes were forbidden in Art. This would account for the surprising dearth of archaeological evidence concerning a cult upon which the very life of mankind was supposed to depend."[10]

In view of the fact that my suggestion as to the possible later development of these Life Cults as Mysteries has aroused considerable opposition, it is well to bear in mind that such development is held by those best acquainted with the earliest forms of the ritual to have been not merely possible, but to have actually taken place, and that at a very remote date. Mr Langdon quotes a passage referring to "Kings who in their day played the *rôle* of Tammuz in the mystery of this cult"; he considers that here we have to do with kings who, by a symbolic act, escaped the final penalty of sacrifice as representative of the Dying God.[11]

The full importance of the evidence above set forth will become more clearly apparent as we proceed with our investigation; here I would simply draw attention to the fact that we now possess definite proof that, at a period of some 3000 years B.C., the idea of a Being upon whose life and reproductive activities the very existence of Nature and its corresponding energies was held to depend, yet who was himself subject to the vicissitudes of declining powers and death, like an ordinary mortal, had already assumed a fixed, and practically final, form; further, that this form was specially crystallized in

10 Cf. Langdon, *op. cit.* p. 24.
11 Cf. Langdon, *op. cit.* p. 26.

ritual observances. In our study of the later manifestations of this cult we shall find that this central
idea is always, and unalterably, the same, and is,
moreover, frequently accompanied by a remarkable
correspondence of detail. The chain of evidence is
already strong, and we may justly claim that the links
added by further research strengthen, while they
lengthen, that chain.

PART II.   ADONIS

While it is only of comparatively recent date that
information as to the exact character of the worship
directed to Tammuz has been available and the material we at present possess is but fragmentary in
character, the corresponding cult of the Phoenician-
Greek divinity we know as Adonis has for some years
been the subject of scholarly research. Not only
have the details of the ritual been examined and discussed, and the surviving artistic evidence described
and illustrated, but from the anthropological side
attention has been forcibly directed to its importance
as a factor in the elucidation of certain widespread
Folk-beliefs and practices.[12]

We know now that the worship of Adonis, which
enjoyed among the Greeks a popularity extending to
our own day, was originally of Phoenician origin, its
principal centres being the cities of Byblos, and

[12] The most complete enquiry into the nature of the god is
to be found in Baudissin, *Adonis und Esmun.* For the details
of the cult cf. Farnell, *Cults of the Greek States,* Vol. II.; Vellay,
Adonis (Annales du Musée Guimet). For the Folk-lore evidence cf. Mannhardt, *Wald und Feld-Kulte;* Frazer, *The
Golden Bough,* and *Adonis, Attis, Osiris.* These remarks apply
also to the kindred cult of Attis, which as we shall see later
forms an important link in our chain of evidence. The two
cults are practically identical and scholars are frequently at
a loss to which group surviving fragments of the ritual should
be assigned.

Aphaka. From Phoenicia it spread to the Greek islands, the earliest evidence of the worship being found in Cyprus, and from thence to the mainland, where it established itself firmly. The records of the cult go back to 700 B.C., but it may quite possibly be of much earlier date. Mr Langdon suggests that the worship of the divinity we know as Adonis, may, under another name, reach back to an antiquity equal with that we can now ascribe to the cult of Tammuz. In its fully evolved classical form the cult of Adonis offers, as it were, a halfway house, between the fragmentary relics of Aryan and Babylonian antiquity, and the wealth of Medieval and Modern survivals to which the ingenuity and patience of contemporary scholars have directed our attention.

We all know the mythological tale popularly attached to the name of Adonis; that he was a fair youth, beloved of Aphrodite, who, wounded in the thigh by a wild boar, died of his wound. The goddess, in despair at his death, by her prayers won from Zeus the boon that Adonis be allowed to return to earth for a portion of each year, and henceforward the youthful god divides his time between the goddess of Hades, Persephone, and Aphrodite. But the importance assumed by the story, the elaborate ceremonial with which the death of Adonis was mourned, and his restoration to life fêted, the date and character of the celebrations, all leave no doubt that the personage with whom we are dealing was no mere favourite of a goddess, but one with whose life and well-being the ordinary processes of Nature, whether animal or vegetable, were closely and intimately concerned. In fact the central figure of these rites, by whatever name he may be called, is the somewhat elusive and impersonal entity, who represents in anthropomorphic form the principle of animate Nature, upon whose preservation, and un-impaired energies, the life of man, directly, and in-directly, depends.[13]

Before proceeding to examine these rites there is one point, to which I have alluded earlier, in another connection, upon which our minds must be quite clear, *i.e.*, the nature of the injury suffered. Writers upon the subject are of one accord in considering the usual account to be but a euphemistic veiling of the truth, while the close relation between the stories of Adonis and Attis, and the practices associated with the cult, place beyond any shadow of a doubt the fact that the true reason for this universal mourning was the cessation, or suspension, by injury or death, of the reproductive energy of the god upon whose virile activity vegetable life directly, and human life indirectly, depended.[14] What we have need to seize and to insist upon is the overpowering influence which the sense of Life, the need for Life, the essential Sanctity of the Life-giving faculty, exercised upon primitive religions. Vellay puts this well when he says: "In fact, the whole religious

[13] In this connection note the extremely instructive remarks of Miss Harrison in the chapter on Herakles in the work referred to above. She points out that the *Eniautos Daimon* never becomes entirely an Olympian, but always retains traces of his 'Earth' origin. This principle is particularly well illustrated by Adonis, who, though admitted to Olympus as the lover of Aphrodite, is yet by his very nature forced to return to the earth, and descend to the realm of Persephone. This agrees well with the conclusion reached by Baudissin (*Adonis und Esmun*, p. 71) that Adonis belongs to "einer Klasse von Wesen sehr unbestimmter Art, die wohl über den Menschen aber unter den grossen Göttern stehen."

[14] Cf. Vellay, *op. cit.* p. 93. Dulaure, *Des Divinités Génératrices*. If Baudissin be correct, and the introduction of the Boar a later addition to the story, it would seem to indicate the intrusion of a phallic element into ritual which at first, like that of Tammuz, dealt merely with the death of the god. The Attis form, on the contrary, appears to have been phallic from the first. Cf. Baudissin, *Adonis und Esmun*, p. 160.

cycle of the Oriental peoples of antiquity rests on
the conception of physical life, considered in its
origin and its action, and in the dual principle which
animates it."[15]

Professor von Schroeder says even more precisely and emphatically: "In the ancient Aryan
religion everything is aimed at the affirmation of life.
The phallus can be considered its dominant symbol."[16] And in spite of the strong opposition to
this cult manifested in Indian literature, beginning
with the *Rig-Veda*, and ripening to fruition in the
Upanishads, in spite of the rise of Buddhism, with
its opposing dictum of renunciation, the 'Life-Cult'
asserted its essential vitality against all opposition,
and under modified forms represents the 'popular'
religion of India to this day.

Each and all of the ritual dramas, reconstructed
in the pages of *Mysterium und Mimus* bear, more
or less distinctly, the stamp of their 'Fertility'
origin,[17] while outside India the pages of Frazer and
Mannhardt, and numerous other writers on Folk-
lore and Ethnology, record the widespread, and
persistent, survival of these rites, and their successful
defiance of the spread of civilization.

It is to this special group of belief and practice
that the Adonis (and more especially its Phrygian
counterpart the Attis) worship belong, and even
when transplanted to the more restrained and cul-
tured environment of the Greek mainland, they
still retained their primitive character. Farnell, in

[15] *Op. cit.* p. 83.
[16] Cf. L. von Schroeder, *Vollendung des Arischen Mysterium,* p. 14.
[17] It may be well to explain the exact meaning attached to
these terms by the author. In Professor von Schroeder's view
Mysterium may be held to connote a drama in which the gods
themselves are actors; *Mimus* on the contrary, is the term
applied to a drama which treats of the doings of mortals.

his *Cults of the Greek States,* refers to the worship
of Adonis as "a ritual that the more austere State
religion of Greece probably failed to purify, the
saner minds, bred in a religious atmosphere that
was, on the whole, genial, and temperate, revolted
from the din of cymbals and drums, the meaningless ecstasies of sorrow and joy, that marked the
new religion."[18]

It is, I submit, indispensable for the purposes of
our investigation that the essential character and
significance of the cults with which we are dealing
should not be evaded or ignored, but faced, frankly
admitted and held in mind during the progress of
our enquiry.

Having now determined the general character
of the ritual, what were the specific details?

The date of the feast seems to have varied in
different countries; thus in Greece it was celebrated
in the Spring, the moment of the birth of Vegetation;
according to Saint Jerome, in Palestine the celebration fell in June, when plant life was in its first
full luxuriance. In Cyprus, at the autumnal equinox,
i.e., the beginning of the year in the Syro-Macedo-
nian calendar, the death of Adonis falling on the 23rd
of September, his resurrection on the 1st of October,
the beginning of a New Year. This would seem to
indicate that here Adonis was considered, as Vellay
suggests, less as the god of Vegetation than as the
superior and nameless Lord of Life (Adonis=Syriac
Adôn, Lord), under whose protection the year was
placed.[19] He is the *Eniautos Daimon.*

[18] *Op. cit.* Vol. ii. p. 647.
[19] *Op. cit.* p. 115. Much of the uncertainty as to date is
doubtless due to the reflective influence of other forms of the
cult; the Tammuz celebrations were held from June 20th, to
July 20th, when the Dog-star Sirius was in the ascendant, and
vegetation failed beneath the heat of the summer sun. In
other, and more temperate, climates the date would fall later.

In the same way as the dates varied, so, also, did the order of the ritual; generally speaking the elaborate ceremonies of mourning for the dead god, and committing his effigy to the waves, preceded the joyous celebration of his resurrection, but in Alexandria the sequence was otherwise; the feast began with the solemn and joyous celebration of the nuptials of Adonis and Aphrodite, at the conclusion of which a Head, of papyrus, representing the god, was, with every show of mourning, committed to the waves, and borne within seven days by a current (always to be counted upon at that season of the year) to Byblos, where it was received and welcomed with popular rejoicing.[20] The duration of the feast varied from two days, as at Alexandria, to seven or eight.

Connected with the longer period of the feast were the so-called 'Gardens of Adonis,' baskets, or pans, planted with quick growing seeds, which speedily come to fruition, and as speedily wither. In the modern survivals of the cult three days form the general term for the flowering of these gardens.[21]

The most noticeable feature of the ritual was the prominence assigned to women; "It is the women who weep for him and accompany him to his tomb. They sob wildly all night long; this is their god more than any other, and they alone wish to lament his death and sing of his resurrection."[22]

Where, however, the cult was an off-shoot of a Tammuz original (as might be the case through emigration) the tendency would be to retain the original date.

[20] Cf. Vellay, *op. cit.* p. 55; Mannhardt, Vol. II. pp. 277–78, for a description of the feast. With regard to the order and sequence of the celebration cf. Miss Harrison's remark, *Themis*, p. 415: "In the cyclic monotony of the *Eniautos Daimon* it matters little whether Death follows Resurrection, or Resurrection, Death."

[21] Cf. Mannhardt, *supra*, p. 279.

[22] Cf. Vellay, *op. cit.* p. 103. This seems also to have been the case with Tammuz, cf. Ezekiel, Chap. viii. *v.* 14.

Thus in the tenth century the festival received the Arabic name of *El-Bûgat,* or 'The Festival of the Weeping Women.'[23]

One very curious practice during these celebrations was that of cutting off the hair in honour of the god; women who hesitated to make this sacrifice must offer themselves to strangers, either in the temple, or on the market-place, the gold received as the price of their favours being offered to the goddess. This obligation only lasted for one day.[24] It was also customary for the priests of Adonis to mutilate themselves in imitation of the god, a distinct proof, if one were needed, of the traditional cause of his death.[25]

Turning from a consideration of the Adonis ritual, its details, and significance, to an examination of the Grail romances, we find that their *mise-en-scène* provides a striking series of parallels with the Classical celebrations, parallels, which instead of vanishing, as parallels have occasionally an awkward habit of doing, before closer investigation, rather gain in force the more closely they are studied.

Thus the central figure is either a dead knight on a bier (as in the *Gawain* versions), or a wounded king on a litter; when wounded the injury corresponds with that suffered by Adonis and Attis.[26]

Closely connected with the wounding of the king is the destruction which has fallen on the land, which will be removed when the king is healed. The version of *Sone de Nansai* is here of extreme interest; the position is stated with so much clearness and precision that the conclusion cannot be evaded—we are

---

[23] Cf. Frazer, *The Golden Bough,* under heading *Adonis.*
[24] Vellay, p. 130; Mannhardt, Vol. ii. p. 287; note the writer's suggestion that the women here represent the goddess, the stranger, the risen Adonis.
[25] Cf. Vellay, p. 93.
[26] *Vide supra,* pp. 20, 21.

face to face with the dreaded calamity which it was the aim of the Adonis ritual to avert, the temporary suspension of all the reproductive energies of Nature.[27]

While the condition of the king is the cause of general and vociferous lamentation, a special feature, never satisfactorily accounted for, is the presence of a weeping woman, or several weeping women. Thus in the interpolated visit of Gawain to the Grail castle, found in the C group of *Perceval* MSS., the Grail-bearer weeps piteously, as she does also in *Diû Crône*.[28]

In the version of the prose *Lancelot* Gawain, during the night, sees twelve maidens come to the door of the chamber where the Grail is kept, kneel down, and weep bitterly, in fact behave precisely as did the classical mourners for Adonis—"They sob wildly all night long."[29]—behaviour for which the text, as it

[27] *Supra*, p. 21.

[28] Cf. Potvin, appendix to Vol. III.; *Sir Gawain at the Grail Castle*, pp. 41, 44 and note.

[29] My use of this parallel has been objected to on the ground that the prose *Lancelot* is a late text, and therefore cannot be appealed to as evidence for original incidents. But the *Lancelot* in its original form was held by so competent an authority as the late M. Gaston Paris to have been one of the earliest, if not the very earliest, of French prose texts. (Cf. M. Paris's review of Suchier and Birch-Hirschfeld's *Geschichte der Franz. Litt.*) The adventure in question is a 'Gawain' adventure; we do not know whence it was derived, and it may well have been included in an early version of the romance. Apart from the purely literary question, from the strictly critical point of view the adventure is here obviously out of place, and entirely devoid of *raison d'être*. If the origin of the Grail legend is really to be found in these cults, which are not a dead but a living tradition (how truly living, the exclusively literary critic has little idea), we are surely entitled to draw attention to the obvious parallels, no matter in which text they appear. I am not engaged in reconstructing the original *form* of the Grail story, but in endeavouring to ascertain the ultimate *source*, and it is surely justifiable to point out that, in effect, no matter what version we take, we find in that

now stands, provides no shadow of explanation or
excuse. The Grail is here the most revered of Christian relics, the dwellers in the castle of Corbenic
have all that heart can desire, with the additional
prestige of being the guardians of the Grail; if the
feature be not a belated survival, which has lost its
meaning, it defies any explanation whatsoever.

In *Diû Crône* alone, where the Grail-bearer and
her maidens are the sole living beings in an abode
of the Dead, is any explanation of the 'Weeping
Women' attempted, but an interpolated passage in
the Heralds' College MS. of the *Perceval* states that
when the Quest is achieved, the hero shall learn the
cause of the maiden's grief, and also the explanation
of the Dead Knight upon the bier:

> "Of the Grail and the maiden's woe,
> He who comes afterwards shall know,
> Why the damsel from the knight's bier
> Bears the Grail with many a tear,
> He shall learn then the truth that none
> Could ever earlier have won."

fo. 180vo–181.

Of course in the *Perceval* there is neither a Weeping Maiden, nor a Bier, and the passage must therefore be either an unintelligent addition by a scribe
familiar with the *Gawain* versions, or an interpolation from a source which did contain the features in
question. So far as the texts at our disposal are concerned, both features belong exclusively to the
Gawain, and not to the *Perceval* Quest. The interpolation is significant as it indicates a surviving sense
of the importance of this feature.

---

version points of contact with one special group of popular
belief and practice. If I be wrong in my conclusions my critics
have only to suggest another origin for this peculiar feature
of the romance—as a matter of fact, they have failed to do so.

In the *Perlesvaus* we have the curious detail of a maiden who has lost her hair as a result of the hero's failure to ask the question, and the consequent sickness of the Fisher King. The occurrence of this detail may be purely fortuitous, but at the same time it is admissible to point out that the Adonis cults do provide us with a parallel in the enforced loss of hair by the women taking part in these rites, while no explanation of this curious feature has so far as I am aware been suggested by critics of the text.[30]

We may also note the fact that the Grail castle is always situated in the close vicinity of water, either on or near the sea, or on the banks of an important river. In two cases the final home of the Grail is in a monastery situated upon an island. The presence of water, either sea, or river, is an important feature in the Adonis cult, the effigy of the dead god being, not buried in the earth, but thrown into the water.[31]

It will thus be seen that, in suggesting a form of Nature worship, analogous to this well-known cult, as the possible ultimate source from which the incidents and *mise-en-scène* of the Grail stories were derived, we are relying not upon an isolated parallel, but upon a group of parallels, which alike in incident and intention offer, not merely a resemblance to, but also an explanation of, the perplexing problems of the Grail literature. We must now consider the question whether incidents so remote in time may fairly and justly be utilized in this manner.

[30] Cf. *Perlesvaus*, Branch ii. Chap. 1.
[31] Throwing into, or drenching with, water is a well-known part of 'Fertility' ritual; it is a case of sympathetic magic, acting as a rain charm.

CHAPTER V

Medieval and Modern Forms of Nature Ritual

READERS of the foregoing pages may, not improbably, object that, while we have instanced certain curious and isolated parallels from early Aryan literature and tradition, and, what, from the point of view of declared intention, appears to be a kindred group of religious belief and practice in pre-Historic and Classical times, the two, so far, show no direct signs of affiliation, while both may be held to be far removed, in point of date, alike from one another, and from the romantic literature of the twelfth century.

This objection is sound in itself, but if we can show by modern parallels that the ideas which took form and shape in early Aryan Drama, and Babylonian and Classic Ritual, not only survive to our day, but are found in combination with features corresponding minutely with details recorded in early Aryan literature, we may hold the gulf to be bridged, and the common origin, and close relationship, of the different stages to be an ascertained fact. At the outset, and before examining the evidence collected by scholars, I would remind my readers that the modern Greeks have retained, in many instances under changed names, no inconsiderable portion of their ancient mythological beliefs, among them the 'Adonis' celebrations; the 'Gardens of Adonis' blossom and fade to-day, as they did many centuries ago, and I have myself spoken with a scholar who has seen 'women, at the door of their houses, weeping for Adonis.'[1]

For evidence of the widespread character of Medieval and Modern survivals we have only to consult the epoch-making works of Mannhardt, *Wald und Feld-Kulte*, and Frazer, *The Golden Bough;*[2] in the pages of these volumes we shall find more than sufficient for our purpose. From the wealth of illustration with which these works abound I have selected merely such instances as seem to apply more directly to the subject of our investigation.[3]

Thus, in many places, it is still the custom to carry a figure representing the Vegetation Spirit on a bier, attended by mourning women, and either bury the figure, throw it into water (as a rain charm), or, after a mock death, carry the revivified Deity, with rejoicing, back to the town. Thus in the Lechrain a man in black women's clothes is borne on a bier, followed by men dressed as professional women mourners making lamentation, thrown on the village dung-heap, drenched with water, and buried in straw.[4]

In Russia the Vegetation or Year Spirit is known as Yarilo,[5] and is represented by a doll with phallic attributes, which is enclosed in a coffin, and carried

[1] *Ancient Greek Religion, and Modern Greek Folk-Lore,* J. C. Lawson, gives some most interesting evidence as to modern survivals of mythological beliefs.

[2] *Wald und Feld-Kulte*, 2nd edition, 2 vols., Berlin, 1904. Cf. Vol. ii. p. 286. *The Golden Bough,* 3rd edition, 5 vols.

[3] I cite from Mannhardt, as the two works overlap in the particular line of research we are following: the same instances are given in both, but the honour of priority belongs to the German scholar.

[4] *Op. cit.* Vol. i. p. 411.

[5] See G. Calderon, 'Slavonic Elements in Greek religion,' *Classical Review,* 1918, p. 79.

through the streets to the accompaniment of lamentation by women whose emotions have been excited by drink. Mannhardt gives the lament as follows: "Of what was he guilty? He was so good! He will never rise again! O! How shall we separate ourselves from you? What does life mean if you are no longer here? Arise, if only for a brief hour! But he does not arise, he does not arise!"[6]

In other forms of the ritual, we find distinct traces of the resuscitation of the Vegetation Deity, occasionally accompanied by evidence of rejuvenation. Thus, in Lausitz, on Laetare Sunday (the 4th Sunday in Lent), women with mourning veils carry a straw figure, dressed in a man's shirt, to the bounds of the next village, where they tear the effigy to pieces, hang the shirt on a young and flourishing tree, "a beautiful forest tree," which they proceed to cut down, and carry home with every sign of rejoicing. Here evidently the young tree is regarded as a rejuvenation of the person represented in the first instance by the straw figure.[7]

In many parts of Europe to-day the corresponding ceremonies, very generally held at Whitsuntide, include the mock execution of the individual representing the Vegetation Spirit, frequently known as the King of the May. In Bohemia the person playing the *rôle* of the King is, with his attendants, dressed in bark, and decked with garlands of flowers; at the conclusion of the ceremonies the King is allowed a short start, and is then pursued by the armed attendants. If he is not overtaken he holds office for a year, but if overtaken, he suffers a mock decapitation, head-dress, or crown, being struck off, and the pretended corpse is then borne on a bier to the next village.[8]

[6] *Op. cit.* p. 416.   [7] *Op. cit.* pp. 155 and 312.
[8] *Op. cit.* p. 353.

Mannhardt, discussing this point, remarks that in the mock execution we must recognize "a wide-spread and certainly an age-old practice." He enumerates the various modes of death, shooting, stabbing (in the latter case a bladder filled with blood, and concealed under the clothes, is pierced); in Bohemia, decapitation, occasionally drowning (which primarily represents a rain charm), is the form adopted.[9] He then goes on to remark that this ceremonial death must have been generally followed by resuscitation, as in Thuringia, where the 'Wild Man,' as the central figure is there named, is brought to life again by the Doctor, while the survival, in the more elaborate Spring processions of this latter character, even where he plays no special *rôle*, points to the fact that his part in the proceedings was originally a more important one.

That Mannhardt was not mistaken is proved by the evidence of the kindred Dances, a subject we shall consider later; there we shall find the Doctor playing his old-time *rôle*, and restoring to life the slain representative of the Vegetation Spirit.[10] The character of the Doctor, or Medicine Man, formed, as I believe, at one time, no unimportant link in the chain which connects these practices with the Grail tradition.

The signification of the resuscitation ceremony is obscured in cases where the same figure undergoes death and revival without any corresponding change of form. This point did not escape Mannhardt's acute critical eye; he remarks that, in cases where, *e.g.*, in Swabia, the 'King' is described as "a poor old man," who has lived seven years in the woods (the seven winter months), a scene of rejuvenation should follow—"this seems for the most part to have been lost,

[9] *Op. cit.* p. 358.
[10] *Op. cit.* p. 358.

but perhaps it only *seems* so." He goes on to draw
attention to the practice in Reideberg, bei Halle,
where, after burying a straw figure, called the Old
Man, the villagers dance round the May-Pole, and he
suggests that the 'Old Man' represents the defunct
Vegetation Spirit, the May Tree, that Spirit resusci-
tated, and refers in this connection to "the completely related Asiatic practices of the Attis and
Adonis cults."[11]

The foregoing evidence offers, I think, sufficient
proof of the, now generally admitted, relationship
between Classical, Medieval, and Modern forms of
Nature ritual.

But what of the relation to early Aryan practice?
Can that, also, be proved?

In this connection I would draw attention to
Chapter 17 of *Mysterium und Mimus,* entitled, *A
Popular Procession at the Festival of Soma.* Here
Professor von Schroeder discusses the real meaning
and significance of a very curious little poem (*Rig-
Veda,* 9. 112); the title by which it is generally
known, *Everyone Runs After Money,* does not, at
first sight, fit the content of the verse, and the suggestion of scholars who have seen in it a humorous
enumeration of different trades and handicrafts does
not explain the fact that the Frog and the Horse
appear in it.

To Professor von Schroeder belongs the credit of
having discovered that the *personnel* of the poem
corresponds with extraordinary exactitude to the
Figures of the Spring and Summer 'Fertility-exciting'
processions, described with such fulness of detail by
Mannhardt. Especially is this the case with the
Whitsuntide procession at Värdegötzen, in Hanover,
where we find the group of phallic and fertility de-

---

[11] *Op. cit.* p. 359. Cf. the Lausitz custom given *supra,* which
Mannhardt seems to have overlooked.

mons, who, on Prof. von Schroeder's hypothesis, figure in the song, in concrete, and actual form.[12] The
Vegetation Spirit appears in the song as an Old Man,
while his female counterpart, an Old Woman, is described as 'filling the hand-mill.' Prof. von Schroeder
points out that in some parts of Russia the 'Baba-
jaga' as the Corn Mother is called, is an Old Woman,
who flies through the air in a hand-mill. The Doctor,
to whom we have referred above, is mentioned twice
in the four verses composing the song; he was evidently regarded as an important figure; while the
whole is put into the mouth of a 'Singer' evidently
the Spokesman of the party, who proclaims their
object, [literally] "knowing different ones, we are
seeking good things," *i.e.*, gifts in money and kind, as
such folk processions do to-day.

The whole study is of extraordinary interest for
Folk-lore students, and so far as our especial investigation is concerned it seems to me to supply the
necessary proof of the identity, and persistence, of
Aryan folk-custom and tradition.

A very important modification of the root idea,
and one which appears to have a direct bearing on
the sources of the Grail tradition, was that by which,
among certain peoples, the *rôle* of the god, his responsibility for providing the requisite rain upon
which the fertility of the land, and the life of the
folk, depended, was combined with that of the King.
This was the case among the Celts; McCulloch, in

---

[12] In the poem, besides the ordinary figures of the Vegetation Deity, his female counterpart, and the Doctor, common
to all such processions, we have Phallus, Frog, and Horse; in
the Folk-procession, Laubfrosch, combining the two first, and
Horse. Cf. Mannhardt, *Mythol. Forsch.* pp. 142–43; *Mysterium und Mimus*, pp. 408 *et seq.*; also, pp. 443–44. Sir W.
Ridgeway (*op. cit.* p. 156) refers slightingly to this interpretation of a 'harmless little hymn'—doubtless the poem is harmless; until Prof. von Schroeder pointed out its close affinity
with the Fertility processions it was also meaningless.

The Religion of the Celts, discussing the question of
the early Irish *geasa* or taboo, explains the *geasa* of
the Irish kings as designed to promote the welfare
of the tribe, the making of rain and sunshine on
which their prosperity depended. "Their observance
made the earth fruitful, produced abundance and
prosperity, and kept both the king and his land from
misfortune. The Kings were divinities on whom depended fruitfulness and plenty, and who must therefore submit to obey their '*geasa.*' "[13]

The same idea seems to have prevailed in early
Greece; Mr A. B. Cook, in his studies on *The European Sky-God,* remarks that the king in early
Greece was regarded as the representative of Zeus:
his duties could be satisfactorily discharged only by
a man who was perfect, and without blemish, *i.e.,* by
a man in the prime of life, suffering from no defect of
body, or mind; he quotes in illustration the speech
of Odysseus (*Od.* 19. 109 ff.). " 'Even as a king without blemish, who ruleth god-fearing over many
mighty men, and maintaineth justice, while the black
earth beareth wheat and barley, and the trees are
laden with fruit, and the flocks bring forth without
fail, and the sea yieldeth fish by reason of his good
rule, and the folk prosper beneath him.' The king
who is without blemish has a flourishing kingdom,
the king who is maimed has a kingdom diseased like
himself, thus the Spartans were warned by an oracle
to beware of a 'lame reign.' "[14]

A most remarkable modern survival of this idea is
recorded by Dr Frazer in the latest edition of *The
Golden Bough,*[15] and is so complete and suggestive
that I make no apology for transcribing it at some
length. The Shilluk, an African tribe, inhabit the

[13] *Op. cit.* Chap. 17, p. 253.
[14] Cf. *Folk-Lore,* Vol. xv. p. 374.
[15] *Op. cit.* Vol. v. *The Dying God,* pp. 17 *et seq.*

banks of the White Nile, their territory extending on the west bank from Kaka in the north, to Lake No in the south, on the east bank from Fashoda to Taufikia, and some 35 miles up the Sohat river. Numbering some 40,000 in all, they are a pastoral people, their wealth consisting in flocks and herds, grain and millet. The King resides at Fashoda, and is regarded with extreme reverence, as being a re-incarnation of Nyakang, the semi-divine hero who settled the tribe in their present territory. Nyakang is the rain-giver, on whom their life and prosperity depend; there are several shrines in which sacred Spears, now kept for sacrificial purposes, are preserved, the originals, which were the property of Nyakang, having disappeared.

The King, though regarded with reverence, must not be allowed to become old or feeble, lest, with the diminishing vigour of the ruler, the cattle should sicken, and fail to bear increase, the crops should rot in the field and men die in ever growing numbers. One of the signs of failing energy is the King's inability to fulfil the desires of his wives, of whom he has a large number. When this occurs the wives report the fact to the chiefs, who condemn the King to death forthwith, communicating the sentence to him by spreading a white cloth over his face and knees during his mid-day slumber. Formerly the King was starved to death in a hut, in company with a young maiden but (in consequence, it is said, of the great vitality and protracted suffering of one King) this is no longer done; the precise manner of death is difficult to ascertain; Dr Seligmann, who was Sir J. G. Frazer's authority, thinks that he is now strangled in a hut, especially erected for that purpose.

At one time he might be attacked and slain by a rival, either of his own family, or of that of one of the previous Kings, of whom there are many, but this has long been superseded by the ceremonial slaying of the monarch who after his death is revered as Nyakang.[16]

This survival is of extraordinary interest; it presents us with a curiously close parallel to the situation which, on the evidence of the texts, we have postulated as forming the basic idea of the Grail tradition—the position of a people whose prosperity, and the fertility of their land, are closely bound up with the life and virility of their King, who is not a mere man, but a Divine re-incarnation. If he 'falls into languishment,' as does the Fisher King in *Perlesvaus,* the land and its inhabitants will suffer correspondingly; not only will the country suffer from drought, "Nor are meadows growing green," but the men will die in numbers:

"Ladies sad will lose their mates"

we may say; the cattle will cease to bear increase:

"And hapless beasts shall bear no young,"

and the people take drastic steps to bring about a rejuvenation; the old King dies, to be replaced by a young and vigorous successor, even as Brons was replaced by Perceval.

Let us now turn back to the preceding chapter, and compare the position of the people of the Shilluk tribe, and the subjects of the Grail King, with that of the ancient Babylonians, as set forth in their Lamentations for Tammuz.

There we find that the absence of the Life-giving deity was followed by precisely the same disastrous consequences;

Vegetation fails—

[16] See Dr Seligmann's study, *The Cult of Nyakang and the Divine Kings of the Shilluk* in the Fourth Report of Wellcome Research Laboratories, Khartum, 1911, Vol. B.

"The wailing is for the plants; the first lament is they
grow not.
The wailing is for the barley; the ears grow not."

The reproductive energies of the animal kingdom
are suspended—

"For the habitation of flocks it is; they produce not.
For the perishing wedded ones, for perishing children it is; the dark-headed people create not."

Nor can we evade the full force of the parallel by
objecting that we are here dealing with a god, not
with a man; we possess the recorded names of 'kings
who played the *rôle* of Tammuz,' thus even for that
early period the commingling of the two conceptions, god and king, is definitely established.

Now in face of this group of parallels, whose close
correspondence, if we consider their separation in
point of time (3000 B.C.; 1200 A.D.; and the present
day), is nothing short of astonishing, is it not absolutely and utterly unreasonable to admit (as scholars
no longer hesitate to do) the relationship between
the first and last, and exclude, as a mere literary invention, the intermediate parallel?

The ground for such a denial may be mere prej-
udice, a reluctance to renounce a long cherished
critical prepossession, but in the face of this new
evidence does it not come perilously close to scientific dishonesty, to a disregard for that respect for
truth in research the imperative duty of which has
been so finely expressed by the late M. Gaston Paris.
—"I profess this doctrine absolutely and without res-
ervation, that knowledge has no other object than
truth, and truth for its own sake, without regard for
the consequences, good or bad, regrettable or fortunate, which this truth can have in practice."[17] When

---

[17] Cf. Address on reception into the Academy when M. Paris
succeeded to Pasteur's *fauteuil*.

we further consider that behind these three main parallels, linking them together, there lies a continuous chain of evidence, expressed alike in classical literature, and surviving Folk practice, I would submit that there is no longer any shadow of a doubt that in the Grail King we have a romantic literary version of that strange mysterious figure whose presence hovers in the shadowy background of the history of our Aryan race; the figure of a divine or semi-divine ruler, at once god and king, upon whose life, and unimpaired vitality, the existence of his land and people directly depends.

And if we once grant this initial fact, and resolve that we will no longer, in the interests of an outworn critical tradition, deny the weight of scientific evidence in determining the real significance of the story, does it not inevitably follow, as a logical sequence, that such versions as fail to connect the misfortunes of the land directly with the disability of the king, but make them dependent upon the failure of the Quester, are, by that very fact, stamped as secondary versions. That by this one detail, of capital importance, they approve themselves as literary treatments of a traditional theme, the true meaning of which was unknown to the author?

Let us for a moment consider what the opposite view would entail; that a story which was originally the outcome of pure literary invention should in the course of re-modelling have been accidentally brought into close and detailed correspondence with a deeply rooted sequence of popular faith and practice is simply inconceivable, the re-modelling, if re-modelling there were, must have been intentional, the men whose handiwork it was were in possession of the requisite knowledge.

But how did they possess that knowledge, and why should they undertake such a task? Surely not

from the point of view of antiquarian interest, as
might be done to-day; they were no twelfth century
Frazers and Mannhardts; the subject must have had
for them a more living, a more intimate, interest.
And if, in face of the evidence we now possess, we
feel bound to admit the existence of such knowledge,
is it not more reasonable to suppose that the men
who first told the story were the men who *knew*, and
that the confusion was due to those who, with more
literary skill, but less first-hand information, remodelled the original theme?

In view of the present facts I would submit that
the problem posed in our first chapter may be held
to be solved; that we accept as a *fait acquis* the conclusion that the woes of the land are directly dependent upon the sickness, or maiming, of the King, and
in no wise caused by the failure of the Quester. The
'Wasting of the land' must be held to have been
antecedent to that failure, and the *Gawain* versions
in which we find this condition fulfilled are, therefore, prior in origin to the *Perceval*, in which the
'Wasting' is brought about by the action of the hero;
in some versions, indeed, has altogether disappeared
from the story.

Thus the position assigned in the versions to this
feature of the Waste Land becomes one of capital
importance as a critical factor. This is a point which
has hitherto escaped the attention of scholars; the
misfortunes of the land have been treated rather as
an accident, than as an essential, of the Grail story,
entirely subordinate in interest to the *dramatis
personae* of the tale, or the objects, Lance and Grail,
round which the action revolves. As a matter of
fact I believe that the 'Waste Land' is really the
very heart of our problem; a rightful appreciation
of its position and significance will place us in possession of the clue which will lead us safely through

the most bewildering mazes of the fully developed
tale.

Since the above pages were written Dr Frazer
has notified the discovery of a second African parallel, equally complete, and striking. In *Folk-Lore*
(Vol. XXVI.) he prints, under the title *A Priest-King
in Nigeria,* a communication received from Mr P. A.
Talbot, District Commissioner in S. Nigeria. The
writer states that the dominant Ju-Ju of Elele, a town
in the N.W. of the Degema district, is a Priest-King,
elected for a term of seven years. "The whole prosperity of the town, especially the fruitfulness of
farm, byre, and marriage-bed, was linked with his
life. Should he fall sick it entailed famine and grave
disaster upon the inhabitants." So soon as a successor
is appointed the former holder of the dignity is
reported to 'die for himself.' Previous to the introduction of ordered government it is admitted that
at any time during his seven years' term of office
the Priest might be put to death by any man sufficiently strong and resourceful, consequently it is
only on the rarest occasions (in fact only one such is
recorded) that the Ju-Ju ventures to leave his compound. At the same time the riches derived from the
offerings of the people are so considerable that there
is never a lack of candidates for the office.

From this and the evidence cited above it would
appear that the institution was widely spread in
Africa, and at the same time it affords a striking
proof in support of the essential soundness of Dr
Frazer's interpretation of the Priest of Nemi, an
interpretation which has been violently attacked in
certain quarters, very largely on the ground that no
one would be found willing to accept an office in-
volving such direct danger to life. The above evidence shows clearly that not only does such an office
exist, but that it is by no means an unpopular post.

CHAPTER VI

The Symbols

In the previous chapters we have discussed the Grail Legend from a general, rather than a specific, point of view; *i.e.*, we have endeavoured to ascertain what was the real character of the task imposed upon the hero, and what the nature and value of his achievement.

We have been led to the conclusion that that achievement was, in the first instance, of an altruistic character—it was no question of advantages, temporal or spiritual, which should accrue to the Quester himself, but rather of definite benefits to be won for others, the freeing of a ruler and his land from the dire results of a punishment which, falling upon the King, was fraught with the most disastrous consequences for his kingdom.

We have found, further, that this close relation between the ruler and his land, which resulted in the ill of one becoming the calamity of all, is no mere literary invention, proceeding from the fertile imagination of a twelfth century court poet, but a deeply rooted popular belief, of practically immemorial antiquity and inexhaustible vitality; we can trace it back thousands of years before the Christian era, we find it fraught with decisions of life and death to-day.

Further, we find in that belief a tendency to express itself in certain ceremonial practices, which retain in a greater or less degree the character of the ritual observances of which they are the survival. Mr E. K. Chambers, in *The Mediaeval Stage*, remarks: "If the comparative study of Religion proves anything it is, that the traditional beliefs and customs of the medieval or modern peasant are in nine cases out of ten but the *detritus* of heathen mythology and heathen worship, enduring with but little external change in the shadow of a hostile faith. This is notably true of the village festivals and their *ludi*. Their full significance only appears when they are regarded as fragments of forgotten cults, the naïve cults addressed by a primitive folk to the beneficent deities of field and wood and river, or the shadowy populace of its own dreams."[1] We may, I think, take it that we have established at least the possibility that in the Grail romances we possess, in literary form, an example of the *detritus* above referred to, the fragmentary record of the secret ritual of a Fertility cult.

Having reached this hypothetical conclusion, our next step must be to examine the Symbols of this cult, the group of mysterious objects which forms the central point of the action, a true understanding of the nature of these objects being as essential for our success as interpreters of the story as it was for the success of the Quester in days of old. We must ask whether these objects, the Grail itself, whether Cup or Dish; the Lance; the Sword; the Stone—one and all invested with a certain atmosphere of awe, credited with strange virtues, with sanctity itself, will harmonize with the proposed solution, will range themselves fitly and fairly within the framework of this hypothetical ritual.

That they should do so is a matter of capital importance; were it otherwise the theory advanced might well, as some of my critics have maintained,

[1] *Op. cit.* Vol. I. p. 94.

'never get beyond the region of ingenious specula-
tion,' but it is precisely upon the fact that this theory
of origin, and so far as criticism has gone, this theory
alone, does permit of a natural and unforced interpretation of these related symbols that I rely as one
of the most convincing proofs of the correctness of
my hypothesis.

Before commencing the investigation there is
one point which I would desire to emphasize, *viz.*,
the imperative necessity for treating the Symbols or
Talismans, call them what we will, on the same principle as we have treated the incidents of the story,
i.e., as a connected whole. That they be not separated the one *from* the other, and made the subject
of independent treatment, but that they be regarded
in their relation the one *to* the other, and that no
theory of origin be held admissible which does not
allow for that relation as a primitive and indispensable factor. It may be the modern tendency to
specialize which is apt to blind scholars to the essential importance of regarding their object of study
as a whole, that fosters in them a habit of focussing
their attention upon that one point or incident of
the story which lends itself to treatment in their
special line of study, and which induces them to
minimize, or ignore, those elements which lie outside
their particular range. But, whatever the cause, it is
indubitable that this method of 'criticism by isolation' has been, and is, one of the main factors which
have operated in retarding the solution of the Grail
problem.

So long as critics of the story will insist on pulling
it into little pieces, selecting one detail here, another
there, for study and elucidation, so long will the
ensemble result be chaotic and unsatisfactory. We
shall continue to have a number of monographs,
more or less scholarly in treatment—one dealing with

the Grail as a Food-providing talisman, and that alone; another with the Grail as a vehicle of spiritual sustenance. One that treats of the Lance as a Pagan weapon, and nothing more; another that regards it as a Christian relic, and nothing less. At one moment the object of the study will be the Fisher King, without any relation to the symbols he guards, or the land he rules; at the next it will be the relation of the Quester to the Fisher King, without any explanation of the tasks assigned to him by the story. The result obtained is always quite satisfactory to the writer, often plausible, sometimes in a measure sound, but it would defy the skill of the most synthetic genius to co-ordinate the results thus obtained, and combine them in one harmonious whole. They are like pieces of a puzzle, each of which has been symmetrically cut and trimmed, till they lie side by side, un-fitting, and un-related.

And we have been pursuing this method for over fifty years, and are still, apparently, content to go on, each devoting attention to the symmetrical perfection of his own little section of the puzzle, quite indifferent to the fact that our neighbour is in possession of an equally neatly trimmed fragment, which entirely refuses to fit in with our own!

Is it not time that we should frankly admit the unsatisfactory results of these years of labour, and honestly face the fact that while we now have at our disposal an immense mass of interesting and suggestive material often of high value, we have failed, so far, to formulate a conclusion which, by embracing and satisfying the manifold conditions of the problem, will command general acceptance? And if this failure be admitted, may not its cause be sought in the faulty method which has failed to recognize in the Grail story an original whole, in which the parts—the action, the actors, the Symbols, the result to be obtained, incident, and intention—stood from the very first in intimate relation the one to the other? That while in process of utilization as a literary theme these various parts have suffered modification and accretion from this, or that, side, the problem of the *ultimate* source remains thereby unaffected?

Such a reversal of method as I suggest will, I submit, not only provide us with a critical solution capable of general acceptance, but it will also enable us to utilize, and appreciate at their due value, the result of researches which at the present moment appear to be mutually destructive the one of the other. Thus, while the purely Folk-lore interpretation of the Grail and Lance excludes the Christian origin, and the theory of the exclusively Christian origin negatives the Folk-lore, the pre-existence of these symbols in a popular ritual setting would admit, indeed would invite, later accretion alike from folk belief and ecclesiastical legend.

We are the gainers by any light that can possibly be thrown upon the process of development of the story, but studies of the separate symbols while they may, and do, afford valuable *data* for determining the character and period of certain accretions, should not be regarded as supplying proof of the origin of the related group.

Reference to some recent studies in the Legend will make my meaning clear. A reviewer of my small *Quest of the Holy Grail* volume remarked that I appeared to be ignorant of Miss Peebles's study *The Legend of Longinus* "which materially strengthens the evidence for the Christian origin."[2] Now this is precisely what, in my view, the study in question, which I knew and possessed, does not do. As

[2] *The Legend of Longinus*, R. J. Peebles (Bryn Mawr College monographs, Vol. ix.).

evidence for the fact that the Grail legend has taken over certain features derived from the popular 'Longinus' story (which, incidentally, no one disputed), the essay is, I hold, sound, and valuable; as affording material for determining the source of the Grail story, it is, on the other hand, entirely without value.

On the principle laid down above no theory which purports to be explanatory of the source of one symbol can be held satisfactory in a case where that symbol does not stand alone. We cannot accept for the Grail story a theory of origin which concerns itself with the Lance, as independent of the Grail. In the study referred to the author has been at immense pains to examine the different versions of the 'Longinus' legend, and to trace its development in literature; in no single instance do we find Longinus and his Lance associated with a Cup or Vase, receptacle of the Sacred Blood.

The plain fact is that in Christian art and tradition Lance and Cup are not associated symbols. The Lance or Spear, as an instrument of the Passion, is found in conjunction with the Cross, Nails, Sponge, and Crown of Thorns, (anyone familar with the wayside Crosses of Catholic Europe will recognize this), not with the Chalice of the Mass.[3] This latter is associated with the Host, or *Agnus Dei*. Still less is the Spear to be found in connection with the Grail in its Food-providing form of a Dish.

No doubt to this, critics who share the views of Golther and Burdach will object, "but what of the

---

[3] I discussed this point with Miss Lucy Broadwood, Secretary of the Folk-Song Society, who has made sketches of these Crosses, and she entirely agrees with me. In my *Quest of the Holy Grail*, pp. 54 *et seq.*, I have pointed out the absolute dearth of ecclesiastical tradition with regard to the story of Joseph and the Grail.

Byzantine Mass? Do we not there find a Spear connected with the Chalice?"[4]

I very much doubt whether we do—the so-called 'Holy Spear' of the Byzantine, and present Greek, liturgy is simply a small silver spear-shaped knife, nor can I discover that it was ever anything else. I have made careful enquiries of liturgical scholars, and consulted editions of Oriental liturgies, but I can find no evidence that the knife (the use of which is to divide the Loaf which, in the Oriental rite, corresponds to the Wafer of the Occidental, in a manner symbolically corresponding to the Wounds actually inflicted on the Divine Victim) was ever other than what it is to-day. It seems obvious, from the method of employment, that an actual Spear could hardly have been used, it would have been an impossibly unwieldy instrument for the purpose.

Nor is the 'procession' in which the elements are carried from the Chapel of the Prothĕsis to the Sanctuary of a public character comparable with that of the Grail castle; the actual ceremony of the Greek Mass takes place, of course, behind a veil. A point of considerable interest, however, is, what caused this difference in the Byzantine liturgy? What were the influences which led to the introduction of a feature unknown to the Western rite? If, as the result of the evidence set forth in these pages, the ultimate origin of the Grail story be finally accepted as deriving from a prehistoric ritual possessing elements of extraordinary persistence and vitality, then the *mise-en-scène* of that story is older than the Byzantine ritual. Students of the subject are well aware that the tradition of ancient pre-Christian rites and ceremonies lingered on in the East long after they had been banished by the more practical genius of the West. It may well prove that so far

[4] Cf. *Litteraturzeitung*, XXIV. (1903), p. 2821.

from the Grail story being a reminiscence of the Byzantine rite, that rite itself has been affected by a ritual of which the Grail legend preserves a fragmentary record.

In my view a Christian origin for Lance and Cup, as associated symbols, has not been made out; still less can it be postulated for Lance and Cup as members of an extended group, including Dish, Sword, and Stone.

On this point Professor Brown's attempt to find in Irish tradition the origin of the Grail symbols is distinctly more satisfactory.[5]

I cannot accept as decisive the solution proposed, which seems to me to be open to much the same criticism as that which would find in the Lance the Lance of Longinus—both are occupied with details, rather than with *ensemble;* both would find their justification as offering evidence of accretion, rather than of origin; neither can provide us with the required *mise-en-scène.*

But Professor Brown's theory is the more sound in that he is really dealing with a group of associated symbols; in his view Lance and Grail alike belong to the treasures of the Tuatha de Danann (that legendary race of Irish ancestors, who were at once gods and kings), and therefore *ab initio* belong together. But while I should, on the whole, accept the affiliation of the two groups, and believe that the treasures of the Tuatha de Danann really correspond to the symbols displayed in the hall of the Grail castle, I cannot consider that the one is the origin of the other. There is one very fundamental difference, the importance of which I cannot ignore, but which, I believe, has hitherto escaped Professor Brown's attention.

The object corresponding to the Grail itself is

[5] Cf. *The Bleeding Lance,* A. C. L. Brown.

the cauldron of the Dagda, "No company ever went from it unthankful" (or 'unsatisfied').[6]

Now this can in no sense be considered as a Cup, or Vase, nor is it the true parallel to a Dish. The connection with the Grail is to be found solely and exclusively in the food-providing properties ascribed to both. But even here the position is radically different; the impression we derive from the Irish text and its analogous parallels is that of size (it is also called a 'tub'), and inexhaustible content, it is a cauldron of plenty.[7] Now, neither of these qualities can be postulated of the Grail; whatever its form, Cup or Dish, it can easily be borne (in uplifted hands, *entre ses mains hautement porte*) by a maiden, which certainly could not be postulated of a cauldron! Nor is there any proof that the Vessel itself contained the food with which the folk of the Grail castle were regaled; the texts rather point to the conclusion that the appearance of the Grail synchronized with a mysterious supply of food of a choice and varied character. There is never any hint that the folk feed *from the Grail;* the only suggestion of such feeding is in the 'Oiste,' by which the father of the Fisher King (or the King himself) is nourished.

In certain texts the separation of the two is clearly brought out; in *Joseph of Arimathea,* for instance, the Fish caught by Brons is to be placed at one end of the table, the Grail at the other. In Gawain's adventure at the Grail castle, in the prose *Lancelot,* as the Grail is carried through the hall "forthwith were the tables replenished with the choicest meats in the world," but the table before Gawain remains

[6] Cf. Brown, *op. cit.* p. 35; also A. Nutt, *Studies in the Legend of the Holy Grail,* p. 184.
[7] Cf. Brown, *Notes on Celtic Cauldrons of Plenty,* p. 237.

void and bare.[8] I submit that while the Grail is in certain phases a food-supplying talisman it is not one of the same character as the cauldrons of plenty; also while the food supply of these latter has the marked characteristic of *quantity,* that of the Grail is remarkable rather for *quality,* its choice character is always insisted upon.

The perusal of Professor Brown's subsequent study, *Notes on Celtic Cauldrons of Plenty and The Land-Beneath-the-Waves,* has confirmed me in my view that these special objects belong to another line of tradition altogether; that which deals with an inexhaustible submarine source of life, examples of which will be found in the 'Sampo' of the Finnish *Kalewala,* and the ever-grinding mills of popular folk-tale.[9] The fundamental idea here seems to be that of the origin of all Life from Water, a very ancient idea, but one which, though akin to the Grail tradition, is yet quite distinct therefrom. The study of this special theme would, I believe, produce valuable results.[10]

On the whole, I am of opinion that the treasures of the Tuatha de Danann and the symbols of the Grail castle go back to a common original, but that they have developed on different lines; in the process of this development one 'Life' symbol has been exchanged for another.[11]

[8] Cf. *Queste,* Malory, Book xiii. Chap. 7, where the effect is the same.

[9] Cf. *Germanische Elben und Götter beim Estenvolke,* L. von Schroeder (Wien, 1906).

[10] I suggested this point in correspondence with Dr Brugger, who agreed with me that it was worth working out.

[11] Before leaving the discussion of Professor Brown's theory, I would draw attention to a serious error made by the author of *The Legend of Longinus.* On p. 191, she blames Professor Brown for postulating the destructive qualities of the Lance, on the strength of 'an unsupported passage' in the 'Mons' MS., whereas the Montpellier text says that the Lance shall

But Lance and Cup (or Vase) were in truth connected together in a symbolic relation long ages before the institution of Christianity, or the birth of Celtic tradition. They are sex symbols of immemorial antiquity and world-wide diffusion, the Lance, or Spear, representing the Male, the Cup, or Vase, the Female, reproductive energy.[12]

Found in juxtaposition, the Spear upright in the Vase, as in the *Bleheris* and *Balin* (both, be it noted, *Gawain*) forms, their signification is admitted by all familiar with 'Life' symbolism, and they are absolutely in place as forming part of a ritual dealing with the processes of life and reproductive vitality.[13]

A most remarkable and significant use of these symbols is found in the ceremonies of the Samurai, the noble warrior caste of Japan. The aspirant was (I am told still is) admitted into the caste at the age of fourteen, when he was given over to the care of a guardian at least fifteen years his senior, to whom he took an oath of obedience, which was sworn upon the Spear. He remained celibate during the period covered by the oath. When the Samurai was held to have attained the degree of responsibility which would fit him for the full duties of a

---

bring peace. Unfortunately, it is this latter version which is unsupported, all the MSS., without even excepting B.N. 1429, which as a rule agrees with Montpellier, give the 'destructive' version.

[12] Cf. Dulaure, *Des Divinités Génératrices*, p. 77. Also additional chapter to last edition by Van Gennep, p. 333; L. von Schroeder, *Mysterium und Mimus*, pp. 279–80, for symbolic use of the Spear. McCulloch, *Religion of the Celts*, p. 302, suggests that it is not impossible that the cauldron=Hindu *yoni*, which of course would bring it into line with the above suggested meaning of the Grail. I think however that the real significance of the cauldron is that previously indicated.

[13] It is interesting to note that this relative position of Lance and Grail lingers on in late and fully Christianized versions; cf. Sommer, *The Quest of the Holy Grail, Romania*, xxxvi. p. 575.

citizen, a second solemn ceremony was held, at which he was released from his previous vows, and presented with the Cup; he was henceforth free to marry, but intercourse with women previous to this ceremony was at one time punishable with death.[14]

That Lance and Cup are, *outside* the Grail story, 'Life' symbols, and have been such from time immemorial, is a fact; why, then, should they not retain that character *inside* the framework of that story? An acceptance of this interpretation will not only be in harmony with the general *mise-en-scène*, but it will also explain finally and satisfactorily, (*a*) the dominant position frequently assigned to the Lance; (*b*) the fact that, while the Lance is borne in procession by a youth, the Grail is carried by a maiden— the sex of the bearer corresponds with the symbol borne.[15]

But Lance and Cup, though the most prominent of the Symbols, do not always appear alone, but are associated with other objects, the significance of which is not always apparent. Thus the Dish, which is sometimes the form assumed by the Grail itself, at other times appears as a *tailléor*, or carving platter of silver, carried in the same procession as the Grail; or there may be two small *tailléors;* finally, a Sword appears in varying *rôles* in the story.

---

[14] My informant on this point was a scholar, resident in Japan, who gave me the facts as within his personal knowledge. I referred the question to Prof. Basil Hall Chamberlain, who wrote in answer that he had not himself met with the practice but that the Samurai ceremonies differed in different provinces, and my informant might well be correct.

[15] This explanation has at least the merit of simplicity as compared with that proposed by the author of *The Legend of Longinus*, pp. 209 *et seq.*, which would connect the feature with an obscure heretical practice of the early Irish church. It would also meet Professor Brown's very reasonable objections, *The Bleeding Lance*, p. 8; cf. also remarks by Baist quoted in foot-note above.

I have already referred to the fact, first pointed out by the late Mr Alfred Nutt,[16] that the four treasures of the Tuatha de Danann correspond generally with the group of symbols found in the Grail romances; this correspondence becomes the more interesting in view of the fact that these mysterious Beings are now recognized as alike Demons of Fertility and Lords of Life. As Mr Nutt subsequently pointed out, the 'Treasures' may well be, Sword and Cauldron certainly are, 'Life' symbols.

Of direct connection between these Celtic objects and the Grail story there is no trace; as remarked above, we have no Irish Folk or Hero tale at all corresponding to the Legend; the relation must, therefore, go back beyond the date of formation of these tales, *i.e.*, it must be considered as one of origin rather than of dependence.

But we have further evidence that these four objects do, in fact, form a special group entirely independent of any appearance in Folk-lore or Romance. They exist to-day as the four suits of the Tarot.

Students of the Grail texts, whose attention is mainly occupied with Medieval Literature, may not be familiar with the word Tarot, or aware of its meaning. It is the name given to a pack of cards, seventy-eight in number, of which twenty-two are designated as the 'Keys.'

These cards are divided into four suits, which correspond with those of the ordinary cards; they are:

Cup (Chalice, or Goblet)—Hearts.
Lance (Wand, or Sceptre)—Diamonds.
Sword—Spades.
Dish (Circles, or Pentangles, the form varies) —Clubs.

[16] Cf. my *Legend of Sir Perceval*, Vol. ii. pp. 314–15, note.

To-day the Tarot has fallen somewhat into disrepute, being principally used for purposes of divination, but its origin, and precise relation to our present playing-cards, are questions of considerable antiquarian interest. Were these cards the direct parents of our modern pack, or are they entirely distinct therefrom?[17]

Some writers are disposed to assign a very high antiquity to the Tarot. Traditionally, it is said to have been brought from Egypt; there is no doubt that parallel designs and combinations are to be found in the surviving decorations of Egyptian temples, notably in the astronomic designs on the ceiling of one of the halls of the palace of Medinet Abou, which is supported on twenty-two columns (a number corresponding to the 'keys' of the Tarot), and also repeated in a calendar sculptured on the southern façade of the same building, under a sovereign of the XXIII dynasty. This calendar is supposed to have been connected with the periodic rise and fall of the waters of the Nile.[18]

The Tarot has also been connected with an ancient Chinese monument, traditionally erected in commemoration of the drying up of the waters of the Deluge by Yao. The face of this monument is divided up into small sections corresponding in size and number with the cards of the Tarot, and bearing characters which have, so far, not been deciphered.

What is certain is that these cards are used to-day by the Gipsies for purposes of divination, and the opinion of those who have studied the subject is

[17] Mr A. E. Waite, who has published a book on the subject, informs me that the 17 cards preserved in the Bibliothèque du Roi (Bibl. Nationale?) as specimens of the work of the painter Charles Gringonneur, are really Tarots.

[18] Falconnier, in a brochure on *Les XXII Lames Hermétiques du Tarot*, gives reproductions of these Egyptian paintings.

that there is some real ground for the popular tradition that they were introduced into Europe by this mysterious people.

In a very interesting article on the subject in *The Journal of the Gipsy-Lore Society*,[19] Mr De la Hoste Ranking examines closely into the figures depicted on the various cards, and the names attached to the suits by the Gipsies. He comes to the conclusion that many of the words are of Sanskrit, or Hindustani, origin, and sums up the result of the internal evidence as follows: "The Tarot was introduced by a race speaking an Indian dialect. The figure known as 'The Pope' shows the influence of the Orthodox Eastern Faith; he is bearded, and carries the Triple Cross. The card called 'The King' represents a figure with the head-dress of a Russian Grand-Duke, and a shield bearing the Polish Eagle. Thus the people who used the Tarot must have been familiar with a country where the Orthodox Faith prevailed, and which was ruled by princes of the status of Grand-Dukes. The general result seems to point to a genuine basis for the belief that the Tarot was introduced into Europe from the East."

As regards the group of symbols in general, Mr W. B. Yeats, whose practical acquaintance with Medieval and Modern Magic is well known, writes: "(1) Cup, Lance, Dish, Sword, in slightly varying forms, have never lost their mystic significance, and are to-day a part of magical operations. (2) The memory kept by the four suits of the Tarot, Cup, Lance, Sword, Pentangle (Dish), is an esoterical notation for fortune-telling purposes."[20]

[19] *Journal of the Gipsy-Lore Society*, Vol. II. New Series, pp. 14–37.
[20] From a private letter. The ultimate object of Magic in all ages was, and is, to obtain control of the sources of Life. Hence, whatever the use of these objects (of which I know nothing), their appearance in this connection is significant.

But if the connection with the Egyptian and Chinese monuments, referred to above, is genuine, the original use of the 'Tarot' would seem to have been, not to foretell the Future in general, but to predict the rise and fall of the waters which brought fertility to the land.

Such use would bring the 'Suits' into line with the analogous symbols of the Grail castle and the treasures of the Tuatha de Danann, both of which we have seen to be connected with the embodiment of the reproductive forces of Nature.

If it is difficult to establish a direct connection between these two latter, it is practically impossible to argue any connection between either group and the 'Tarot'; no one has as yet ventured to suggest the popularity of the works of Chrétien de Troyes among the Gipsies! Yet the correspondence can hardly be fortuitous. I would suggest that, while Lance and Cup, in their associated form, are primarily symbols of Human Life energy, in conjunction with others they formed a group of 'Fertility' symbols, connected with a very ancient ritual, of which fragmentary survivals alone have been preserved to us.

This view will, I believe, receive support from the evidence of the ceremonial Dances which formed so important a part of 'Fertility' ritual, and which survive in so many places to this day. If we find these symbols reappearing as a part of these dances, their real significance can hardly be disputed.

CHAPTER VII

The Sword Dance

THE subject we are now about to consider is one which of late years has attracted considerable attention, and much acute criticism has been expended on the question of its origin and significance. Valuable material has been collected, but the studies, so far, have been individual, and independent, the much needed *travail d'ensemble* has not yet appeared.

One definite result has, however, been obtained; it is now generally admitted that the so-called Sword Dances, with the closely related Morris Dances, and Mumming Plays, are not mere survivals of martial exercises, an inherited tradition from our warrior ancestors, but were solemn, ceremonial (in some cases there is reason to believe, Initiatory) dances, performed at stated seasons of the year, and directly and intimately connected with the ritual of which we have treated in previous chapters, a ritual designed to preserve and promote the regular and ordered sequence of the processes of Nature. And here, again, our enquiry must begin with the very earliest records of our race, with the traditions of our Aryan forefathers.

The earliest recorded Sword Dancers are undoubtedly the Maruts, those swift-footed youths in gleaming armour who are the faithful attendants on the great god, Indra. Professor von Schroeder, in *Mys-*

terium und Mimus, describes them thus:[1] they are a group of youths of equal age and identical parentage, they are always depicted as attired in the same manner, "They are richly and splendidly adorned, with ornaments of gold on their breasts and bracelets on their arms; they wear deerskins on their shoulders. Above all, they are equipped for war; they carry shining spears in their hands, or golden axes. They are covered with golden armour or cloaks, and helmets of gold gleam on their heads. They never appear without being fully armed. It seems as though their weapons are wholly and entirely part of their being."

The writer goes on to remark that when such a band of armed youths, all of the same age, always closely associated with each other, are represented as Dancers, and always as Dancers—"then, undeniably, we have before our eyes the picture of a war-dance"—and Professor von Schroeder is undoubtedly right.

Constantly throughout the *Rig-Veda* the Maruts are referred to as Dancers, "gold-bedecked Dancers," "with songs of praise they danced round the spring," "When ye Maruts spear-armed dance, they (*i.e.,* the Heavens) stream together like waves of water."[2]

And a special moment for the dance of these glorious youths "ever young brothers of whom none is elder, none younger"[3] is that of the ceremonial sacrifice, "they dance on their heavenly paths; they leap and dance also at the sacrificial feasts of men."[4]

The Maruts, as said above, were conceived of as the companions of Indra, and helpers in his fight

[1] *Mysterium und Mimus,* p. 50. This work contains a most valuable and interesting study of the Maruts, and the kindred groups of Sword Dancers.

[2] *Op. cit.* pp. 47 *et seq.*

[3] *Rig-Veda,* Vol. III. p. 337.

[4] *Mysterium und Mimus,* p. 48.

against his monstrous adversaries; thus they were included in the sacrifices offered in honour of that Deity.

One of the most striking of the ritual Dramas reconstructed by Professor von Schroeder is that which represents Indra as indignantly rejecting the claim of the Maruts to share in such a sacrifice; they had failed to support him in his conflict with the dragon, Vṛitra, when by his might he loosed the waters, 'neither to-day, nor to-morrow' will he accept a sacrifice of which they share the honour; it requires all the tact of the Offerer, Agastya, and of the leader of the Maruts to soothe the offended Deity.[5]

Here I would draw attention to the significant fact that the feat celebrated is that to which I have previously referred as the most famous of all the deeds attributed to Indra, the 'Freeing of the Waters,' and here the Maruts are associated with the god.

But they were also the objects of independent worship. They were specially honoured at the Câturmâsya, the feasts which heralded the commencement of the three seasons of four months each into which the Indian year was divided, a division corresponding respectively to the hot, the cool, and the wet, season. The advantages to be derived from the worship of the Maruts may be deduced from the following extracts from the *Rig-Veda*, which devotes more than thirty hymns to their praise. "The adorable Maruts, armed with bright lances, and cuirassed with golden breastplates, enjoy vigorous existence; may the cars of the quick-moving Maruts arrive for our good." "Bringers of rain and fertility, shedding water, augmenting food." "Givers of abundant food." "Your milchkine are never dry."

[5] *Op. cit., Indra, die Maruts, und Agastya,* pp. 91 *et seq.*

"We invoke the food-laden chariots of the Maruts."[6] Nothing can be clearer than this; the Maruts are 'daimons' of fertility, the worship of whom will secure the necessary supply of the fruits of the earth.

The close association of the Maruts with Indra, the great Nature god, has led some scholars to regard them as personifications of a special manifestation of Nature, as Wind-gods. Professor von Schroeder points out that their father was the god Rudra, later known as Çiva, the god of departed souls, and of fruitfulness, *i.e.*, a Chthonian deity, and suggests that the Maruts represent "a band of spirits hunting in the wind and storm."[7] He points out that the belief in a troop of departed souls is an integral part of Aryan tradition, and classifies such belief under four main headings.

1. Under the form of a spectral Hunt, the Wild Huntsman well known in European Folk-lore. He equates this with Dionysus Zagreus, and the Hunt of Artemis-Hekate.

2. That of a spectral Army, the souls of warriors slain in fight. The Northern *Einherier* belong to this class, and the many traditions of spectral combats, and ghostly battles, heard, but not seen.

3. The conception of a host of women in a condition of ecstatic exaltation bordering on madness, who appear girdled with snakes, or hissing like snakes, tear living animals to pieces, and devour the flesh. The classic examples here are the Greek Maenads, and the Indian Senâs, who accompany Rudra.

4. The conception of a train of theriomorphic, phallic, demons of fertility, with their companion group of fair women. Such are the Satyrs and

[6] *Rig-Veda*, Vol. iii. pp. 331, 334, 335, 337.
[7] *Mysterium und Mimus*, p. 121.

Nymphs of Greek, the Gandharvas and Apsaras of Indian, Mythology.

To these four main groups may be added the belief among Germanic peoples, also among the Letts, in a troop of Child Souls.

These four groups, in more or less modified forms, appear closely connected with the dominant Spirit of Vegetation, by whatever name that spirit may be known.

According to von Schroeder there was, among the Aryan peoples generally, a tendency to regard the dead as assuming the character of daimons of fertility. This view the learned Professor considers to be at the root of the annual celebrations in honour of the Departed, the 'Feast of Souls,' which characterized the commencement of the winter season, and is retained in the Catholic conception of November as the month of the Dead.[8]

In any case we may safely conclude that the Maruts, represented as armed youths, were worshipped as deities of fruitfulness; that their dances were of a ceremonial character; and that they were, by nature and origin, closely connected with spirits of fertility of a lower order, such as the Gandharvas. It also appears probable that, if the Dramas of which traces have been preserved in the *Rig-Veda*, were, as scholars are now of opinion, once actually represented, the mythological conception of the Maruts must have found its embodiment in youths, most probably of the priestly caste, who played their *rôle*, and actually danced the ceremonial Sword Dance. As von Schroeder says, "There is no doubt

---

[8] *Vollendung des Arische Mysterium*, p. 13. The introductory section of this book, containing a study of early Aryan belief, and numerous references to modern survivals, is both interesting and valuable. The latter part, a panegyric on the Wagnerian drama, is of little importance.

that this was performed by human, specifically by priestly persons."[9]

When we turn from the early Aryan to the classic Greek period we find in the Kouretes, and in a minor degree in the Korybantes, a parallel so extraordinarily complete, alike in action and significance, that an essential identity of origin appears to be beyond doubt.

The Kouretes were, as their name indicates, a band of armed youths, of semi-divine origin, "The Kouretes are by origin semi-divine, demoniac beings, not just human priests or their mythical representatives."[10] Again, they are to be considered as "elemental and primitive beings," and as such of "divine origin."[11] Preller regards them as "mountain-demons,"[12] while a passage from Hesiod, quoted by Strabo, equates them with nymphs and satyrs, *i.e.*, fertility demons.[13]

When we remember that the Gandharvas are the Indian equivalent of the Satyrs the close parallel between the Maruts and the Kouretes, both alike bands of armed youths, of elementary origin, and connected with beings of a lower grade, is striking.

The home of the Kouretes was in Crete, where they were closely associated with the worship of the goddess Rhea. The traditional story held that, in order to preserve the infant Zeus from destruction by his father Kronos, they danced their famous Sword Dance round the babe, overpowering his cries by the clash of their weapons.

Their dance was by some writers identified with the Pyrrhic dance, first performed by Athene, in

[9] *Mysterium und Mimus*, p. 131.
[10] Cf. Röscher's *Lexikon*, under heading *Kureten*.
[11] *Op. cit.*
[12] Cf. Preller, *Graechische Mythologie*, p. 134.
[13] Quoted by Preller, p. 654.

honour of her victory over the Giants, and taught by her to the Kouretes. It had however, as we shall see, a very distinct aim and purpose, and one in no way connected with warlike ends.

In Miss J. E. Harrison's deeply interesting volume, *Themis*,[14] she gives the translation of a fragmentary *Hymn of the Kouretes*, discovered among the ruins of a temple in Crete, a text which places beyond all doubt the fact that, however mythical in origin, the Kouretes, certainly, had actual human representatives, and that while in the case of the Maruts there may be a question as to whether their dance actually took place, or not, so far as the Kouretes are concerned there can be no such doubt.

The following is the text as preserved to us; the slabs on which it is inscribed are broken, and there are consequent lacunae.

"Io, Kouros most great, I give thee hail, Kronian, lord of all that is wet and gleaming, thou art come at the head of thy Daimones. To Dikte for the year, Oh march, and rejoice in the dance and song,

"That we make to thee with harps and pipes mingled together, and sing as we come to a stand at thy well-fenced altar.

"Io, &c.

"For here the shielded Nurturers took thee, a child immortal, from Rhea, and with noise of beating feet hid thee away.

"Io, &c.

"And the Horai began to be fruitful year by year, and Dikè to possess mankind and all wild living things were held about by wealth-loving Peace.

"Io, &c.

"To us also leap for full jars, and leap for fleecy

14 *Themis, A Study in Greek Social Origins* (Cambridge, 1912), pp. 6 *et seq.*

flocks, and leap for fields of fruit, and for hives to bring increase.

"Io, &c.

"Leap for our cities, and leap for our sea-borne ships, and leap for our young citizens, and for goodly Themis."

This hymn is extraordinarily interesting; it places beyond all doubt what was the root intention of this ceremonial dance; it was designed to stimulate the reproductive energies of Nature, to bring into being fruitful fields, and vineyards, plenteous increase in the flocks and herds, and to people the cities with youthful citizens; and the god is entreated not merely to accept the worship offered, but himself to join in the action which shall produce such fair results, to leap for full jars, and fleecy flocks, and for youthful citizens.

The importance of movement, notably of what we may call group movement, as a stimulant to natural energies, is thoroughly recognized among primitive peoples; with them Dance holds a position equivalent to that which, in more advanced communities, is assigned to Prayer. Professor von Schroeder comments on this, "It is remarkable to see how, according to the belief of primitive peoples, the dance seems to have a power and significance similar to that which, at higher stages of culture, is attributed to devout prayer."[15] He cites the case of the Tarahumara Indians of Central America; while the family as a whole are labouring in the fields it is the office of one man to dance uninterruptedly on the dance place of the house; if he fails in his office the labour of the others will be unsuccessful. The one sin of which a Tarahumara Indian is conscious is that of not having danced enough. Miss Harrison, in commenting on the dance of the Kour-

[15] *Mysterium und Mimus*, p. 23.

etes, remarks that among certain savage tribes when
a man is too old to dance he hands on his dance
to another. He then ceases to exist socially; when he
dies his funeral is celebrated with scanty rites; having 'lost his dance' he has ceased to count as a social
unit.[16]

With regard to the connection of the Kouretes
with the infant Zeus, Miss Harrison makes the
interesting suggestion that we have here a trace
of an Initiation Dance, analogous to those discussed
by M. Van Gennep in his *Rites du Passage*, that the
original form was Tītăns, 'White-clay men,' which
later became Tītăns, 'Giants,' and she draws attention to the fact that daubing the skin with white clay
is a frequent practice in these primitive rituals. To
this I would add that it is a noteworthy fact that
in our modern survivals of these dances the performers are, as a rule, dressed in white.

The above suggestion is of extreme significance,
as it brings out the possibility that these celebrations
were not only concerned with the prosperity of the
community, as a whole, but may also have borne
a special, and individual, aspect, and that the idea
of Initiation into the group is closely connected
with the ceremonial exercise of group functions.

To sum up, there is direct proof that the classic
Greeks, in common with their Aryan forefathers,
held the conception of a group of Beings, of mythic
origin, represented under the form of armed youths,
who were noted dancers, and whose activities were
closely connected with the processes of Nature. They
recognized a relation between these beings, and
others of a less highly developed aspect, phallic
demons, often of theriomorphic form. Thus the
dance of the Kouretes should be considered as a
ceremonial ritual action, rather than as a warlike

[16] *Themis*, p. 24.

exercise; it was designed to promote the fruitfulness of the earth, not to display the skill of the dancers in the handling of weapons. When we turn to an analogous group, that of the Korybantes, we find that, while presenting a general parallel to the Kouretes (with whom they are often coupled in mythologies), they also possess certain distinct characteristics, which form a connecting link with other, and later, groups.

The Korybantes were of Phrygian origin, attached to the worship of the goddess Kybele, and Attis, the well-known Phrygian counterpart to the Phoenician Adonis, and originally the most important embodiment of the Vegetation Spirit. Röscher considers them to be of identical origin with the Kouretes, *i.e.*, as elementary 'daimons,' but the Korybantes of Classic art and tradition are undoubtedly human beings. Priests of Kybele, they appear in surviving bas-reliefs in company with that goddess, and with Attis.

The dance of the Korybantes is distinguished from that of the Kouretes by its less restrained, and more orgiastic character; it was a wild and whirling dance resembling that of the modern Dervishes, accompanied by self-mutilation and an unrhythmic clashing of weapons, designed, some writers think, to overpower the cries of the victims.

If this suggestion be correct it would seem to indicate that, if the Dance of the Kouretes was originally an Initiation Dance, that of the Korybantes was Sacrificial in character. We shall see later that certain features in the surviving forms of the Sword Dance also point in this direction.

The interest of the Korybantes for our investigation lies in the fact that here again we have the Sword Dance in close and intimate connection with the worship of the Vegetation Spirit, and there

can be no doubt that here, as elsewhere, it was
held to possess a stimulating virtue.

A noticeable point in the modern survivals of
these Dances is that the Dance proper is combined
with a more or less coherent dramatic action. The
Sword Dance originally did not stand alone, but
formed part of a Drama, to the action of which it
may be held to have given a cumulative force.

On this point I would refer the reader to Professor von Schroeder's book, where this aspect of the
Dance is fully discussed.[17]

We have already spoken of the Maruts, and their
dramatic connection with Indra; the Greek Dancers
offer us no direct parallel, though the connection
of the Kouretes with the infant Zeus may quite
possibly indicate the existence in the original form
of the Dance, of a more distinctly dramatic element.

We have, however, in the Roman Salii a connecting link which proves beyond all doubt that our
modern dances, and analogous representations, are
in fact genuine survivals of primitive ceremonies,
and in no way a mere fortuitous combination of
originally independent elements.

The Salii formed a college of priests, twelve in
number, dedicated to the service of Mars, who, it
is important to remember, was originally a god of
growth and vegetation, a Spring Deity, who bestowed his name on the vernal month of March;
only by degrees did the activities of the god become
specially connected with the domain of War.[18]

There seem to have been two groups of Salii, one

[17] Cf. *Mysterium und Mimus,* section *Indra, die Maruts,
und Agastya* specially pp. 151 *et seq.*

[18] Cf. von Schroeder, *op. cit.* pp. 141 *et seq.* for a very full
account of the ceremonies; also, *Themis,* p. 194; Mannhardt,
Wald und Feld-Kulte, and Röscher's *Lexikon,* under heading
Mars, for various references.

having their college on the Palatine, the other on the Quirinal; the first were the more important. The Quirinal group shared in the celebrations of the latter part of the month only.

The first of March was the traditional birthday of Mars, and from that date, during the whole of the month, the Salii offered sacrifices and performed dances in his honour. They wore pointed caps, or helmets, on their head, were girt with swords, and carried on the left arm shields, copied from the 'ancilia' or traditional shield of Mars, fabled to have fallen from heaven. In their right hand they bore a small lance.

Dionysus of Halicarnassus, in a passage describing the Salii, says, "they carried in their right hand a spear, or staff, or something of that sort." Miss Harrison, quoting this passage, gives a reproduction of a bas-relief representing the Salii carrying what she says "are clearly drumsticks." (As a matter of fact they very closely resemble the 'Wands' which in the Tarot cards sometimes represent the 'Lance' suit.)

Miss Harrison suggests that the original shields were made of skins, stretched upon a frame, and beaten by these 'drumsticks.' This may quite well have been the case, and it would bear out my contention that the original contact of weapon and shield was designed rather as a rhythmic accompaniment to the Dance, than as a display of skill in handling sword and lance, *i.e.*, that these dances were not primarily warlike exercises.

At the conclusion of their songs the Salii invoked Mamurius Veturius, the smith who was fabled to have executed the copies of the original shield, while on the 14th of March, a man, dressed in skins, and supposed to represent the aforesaid smith, was led through the streets, beaten by the Salii with rods, and thrust out of the city.

The following day, the 15th, was the feast of Anna Perenna, fabled to be an old woman, to whom Mars had confided the tale of his love for Nerio, and who, disguising herself as the maiden, had gone through the ceremony of marriage with the god. This feast was held outside the gates. On the 23rd the combined feast of Mars and Nerio was held with great rejoicing throughout the city. Modern scholars have unanimously recognized in Mamurius Veturius and Anna Perenna the representatives of the Old Year, the Vegetation Spirit, and his female counterpart, who, grown old, must yield place to the young god and his correspondingly youthful bride. Reference to Chapter 5, where the medieval and modern forms of this Nature ritual are discussed, and instances of the carrying out of Winter, and ceremonial bringing in of Spring, are given, will suffice to show how vital and enduring an element in Folk-lore is this idea of driving out the Old Year, while celebrating the birth of the New. Here then, again, we have a ritual Sword Dance closely associated with the practice of a Nature cult; there can, I think, be no doubt that *ab initio* the two were connected with each other.

But the dance of the Salii with its dramatic Folkplay features forms an interesting link between the classic Dance of the Kouretes, and the modern English survivals, in which the dramatic element is strongly marked. These English forms may be divided into three related groups, the Sword Dance, the Morris Dance, and the Mumming Play. Of these the Morris Dance stands somewhat apart; of identical origin, it has discarded the dramatic element, and now survives simply as a Dance, whereas the Sword Dance is always dramatic in form, and the Mumming Play, acted by characters appearing also in the

Sword Dance, invariably contains a more or less elaborate fight.[19]

The Sword Dance proper appears to have been preserved mostly in the North of England, and in Scotland. Mr Cecil Sharp has found four distinct varieties in Yorkshire alone. At one time there existed a special variant known as the *Giants' Dance,* in which the leading characters were known by the names of Wotan, and Frau Frigg; one figure of this dance consisted in making a ring of swords round the neck of a lad, without wounding him.

Mr E. K. Chambers has commented on this as the survival of a sacrificial origin.[20] The remarks of this writer on the Sword Dance in its dramatic aspect are so much to the point that I quote them here. "The Sword Dance makes its appearance, not like heroic poetry in general, as part of the minstrel repertory, but as a purely popular thing at the agricultural festivals. To these festivals we may therefore suppose it to have originally belonged." Mr Chambers goes on to remark that the dance of the Salii discussed above, was clearly agricultural, "and belongs to Mars not as War god, but in his more primitive quality of a fertilization Spirit."

In an Appendix to his most valuable book the same writer gives a full description, with text, of the most famous surviving form of the Sword Dance, that of Papa Stour (old Norwegian *Pâpey in Stôra*), one of the Shetland Islands.

The dance was performed at Christmas (Yuletide). The dancers, seven in number, represented the seven champions of Christendom; the leader, Saint George, after an introductory speech, performed a

---

[19] *Folk-Lore,* Vols. viii., x., and xvi. contain interesting and fully illustrated accounts of some of these dances and plays.

[20] *The Mediaeval Stage,* Vol. iii. p. 202. It would be interesting to know the precise form of this ring; was it the Pentangle?

solo dance, to the music of an accompanying minstrel. He then presented his comrades, one by one, each in turn going through the same performance. Finally the seven together performed an elaborate dance. The complete text of the speeches is given in the Appendix referred to.[21]

The close connection between the English Sword Dance, and the Mumming Play, is indicated by the fact that the chief character in these plays is, generally speaking, Saint George. (The title has in some cases become corrupted into *King* George.) In Professor von Schroeder's opinion this is due to Saint George's legendary *rôle* as Dragon slayer, and he sees in the importance assigned to this hero an argument in favour of his theory that the "Slaying of the Dragon" was the earliest Aryan Folk-Drama.

In *Folk-Lore*, Vol. x., a fully illustrated description of the Mumming Play, as performed at Newbold, a village near Rugby, is given.[22] Here the characters are Father Christmas, Saint George, a Turkish Knight, Doctor, Moll Finney (mother of the Knight), Humpty Jack, Beelzebub, and 'Big-Head-and-Little-Wit.' These last three have no share in the action proper, but appear in a kind of Epilogue, accompanying a collection made by Beelzebub.

The Play is always performed at Christmas time, consequently Father Christmas appears as stage-manager, and introduces the characters. The action consists in a general challenge issued by Saint George, and accepted by the Turkish Knight. A combat follows, in which the Turk is slain. His mother rushes in, weeps over the body, and demands the services of a Doctor, who appears accordingly, vaunts his skill in lines interspersed with unintel-

[21] Cf. also *Mysterium und Mimus,* pp. 110, 111, for a general description of the dance, *minus* the text of the speeches.
[22] Pp. 186–194.

ligible gibberish, and restores the Turk to life. In the version which used to be played throughout Scotland at Hogmanay (New-Year-tide), the characters are Bol Bendo, the King of France, the King of Spain, Doctor Beelzebub, Golishan, and Sir Alexander.[23] The fight is between Bol Bendo (who represents the Saint George of the English version), and Golishan. The latter is killed, and, on the demand of Sir Alexander (who acts as stage-manager), revived by the doctor, this character, as in the English version, interlarding the recital of his feats of healing skill with unintelligible phrases. [24] There is a general consensus of opinion among Folk-lore authorities that in this rough drama, which we find played in slightly modified form all over Europe (in Scandinavia it is the Julbock, a man dressed in skins, who, after a dramatic dance, is killed and revived),[25] we have a symbolic representation of the death and rebirth of the year; a counterpart to those ceremonies of driving out Winter, and bringing in Spring, which we have already described.

This chapter had already been written when an important article, by Dr Jevons, entitled *Masks and the Origin of the Greek Drama* appeared in *Folk-Lore* (Vol. XXVII.). The author, having discussed the different forms of Greek Drama, and the variety of masks employed, decides that "Greek Comedy originated in Harvest Festivals, in some ceremony in which the Harvesters went about in procession wear-

[23] Cf. *Folk-Lore*, Vol. XVI. pp. 212 *et seq*.

[24] I would draw attention to the curious name of the adversary, Golishan; it is noteworthy that in one Arthurian romance Gawain has for adversary Golagros, in another Percival fights against Golerotheram. Are these all reminiscences of the giant Goliath, who became the synonym for a dangerous, preferably heathen, adversary, even as Mahomet became the synonym for an idol?

[25] Cf. Mannhardt, *Wald und Feld-Kulte*, Vol. II. pp. 191 *et seq*. for a very full account of the Julbock (Yule Buck).

ing masks." This ceremony he connects directly with the English Mumming Plays, suggesting that "the characters represented on this occasion were the Vegetation Spirit, and those who were concerned in bringing about his revivification—in fine, Greek Comedy and the Mumming Play both sprang from the rite of revivification." At a later stage of our enquiry we shall have occasion to return to this point, and realize its great importance for our theory.

The Morris Dances differ somewhat from the Sword, and Mumming Dances. The performances as a rule take place in the Spring, or early Summer, chiefly May, and Whitsuntide. The dances retain little or no trace of dramatic action but are dances pure and simple. The performers, generally six in number, are attired in white elaborately-pleated shirts, decked with ribbons, white mole-skin trousers, with bells at the knee, and beaver hats adorned with ribbons and flowers. The leader carries a sword, on the point of which is generally impaled a cake; during the dancing slices of this cake are distributed to the lookers on, who are supposed to make a contribution to the 'Treasury,' a money-box carried by an individual called the Squire, or Clown, dressed in motley, and bearing in the other hand a stick with a bladder at one end, and a cow's tail at the other.

In some forms of the dance there is a 'Lord' and a 'Lady,' who carry 'Maces' of office; these maces are short staves, with a transverse piece at the top, and a hoop over it. The whole is decorated with ribbons and flowers, and bears a curious resemblance to the *Crux Ansata*.[26] In certain figures of the dance the performers carry handkerchiefs, in others, wands, painted with the colours of the village to which they

[26] Cf. *Folk-Lore*, Vol. VIII. 'Some Oxfordshire Seasonal Festivals,' where full illustrations of the Bampton Morris Dancers and their equipment will be found.

belong; the dances are always more or less elaborate in form.

The costume of the 'Clown' (an animal's skin, or cap of skin with tail pendant) and the special character assumed by the Maytide celebrations in certain parts of England, *e.g.*, Cornwall and Staffordshire,[27] would seem to indicate that, while the English Morris Dance has dropped the dramatic action, the dancers not being designated by name, and playing no special *rôle*, it has, on the other hand, retained the theriomorphic features so closely associated with Aryan ritual, which the Sword Dance, and Mumming Play, on their side, have lost.[28]

A special note of these English survivals, and one to which I would now draw attention, is the very elaborate character of the figures, and the existence of a distinct symbolic element. I am informed that the Sword dancers of to-day always, at the conclusion of a series of elaborate sword-lacing figures, form the Pentangle; as they hold up the sign they cry, triumphantly, *"A Nut! A Nut!"* The word *Nut=Knot* (as in the game of 'Nuts, *i.e.*, breast-knots, nosegays, *in May'*). They do this often even when performing a later form of the Mumming Play.

I have already drawn attention to the fact that in *Gawain and the Green Knight* the hero's badge is the Pentangle (or Pentacle), there explained as called by the English 'the Endless Knot.'[29] In the previous chapter I have noted that the Pentangle frequently in the Tarot suits replaces the Dish; in Mr Yeats's remarks, cited above, the two are held to be interchangeable, one or the other always forms one of the group of symbols.

[27] Cf. *The Padstow Hobby-Horse, F.-L.* Vol. xvi. p. 56; *The Staffordshire Horn-Dance, Ib.* Vol. vii. p. 382, and viii. p. 70.
[28] Cf. *supra*, pp. 56, 84, 89.
[29] Cf. *Legend of Sir Perceval*, Vol. ii. p. 264.

In one form of the Morris Dance, that performed
in Berkshire, the leader, or 'Squire' of the Morris
carries a Chalice! At the same time he bears a Sword,
and a bull's head at the end of a long pole. This
figure is illustrated in Miss Mary Neal's *Esperance
Morris Book*.[30]

Thus our English survivals of these early Vegetation ceremonies preserve, in a more or less detached
form, the four symbols discussed in the preceding
chapter, Grail, Sword, Lance, and Pentangle, or
Dish. It seems to me that, in view of the evidence
thus offered, it is not a very hazardous, or far-fetched
hypothesis to suggest that these symbols, the exact
value of which, as a group, we cannot clearly determine, but of which we know the two most prominent, Cup and Lance, to be sex symbols, were originally 'Fertility' emblems, and as such employed in a
ritual design to promote, or restore, the activity of
the reproductive energies of Nature.

As I have pointed out above an obvious dislocation
has taken place in our English survivals. Sword
Dance, Mumming Play, and Morris Dance, no longer
form part of one ceremony, but have become separated, and connected, on the one hand with the Winter, on the other with the early Summer, Nature
celebrations; it is thus not surprising that the symbols should also have become detached. The fact
that the three groups manifestly form part of an
original whole is an argument in favour of the view
that at one moment all the symbols were used together, and the Grail chalice carried in a ceremony

[30] See *English Folk-Song and Dance* by Frank Kidson and
Mary Neal, Cambridge, 1915, plate facing p. 104. A curious
point in connection with the illustration is that the Chalice is
surmounted by a Heart, and in the Tarot suits *Cups* are the
equivalent of our *Hearts*. The combination has now become
identified with the cult of the Sacred Heart, but is undoubtedly very much older.

in which Sword, Lance, and Pentangle, were also displayed.

But there is another point I would suggest. Is it not possible that, in these armed youths, who were in some cases, notably in that of the Salii, at once warriors and priests, we have the real origin of the Grail Knights? We know now, absolutely, and indubitably, that these Sword Dances formed an inportant part of the Vegetation ritual; is it not easily within the bounds of possibility that, as the general ceremonial became elevated, first to the rank of a Mystery Cult, and then used as a vehicle for symbolic Christian teaching, the figures of the attendant warrior-priests underwent a corresponding change? From Salii to Templars is not after all so 'far a cry' as from the glittering golden-armed Maruts, and the youthful leaping Kouretes, to the grotesque tatter-demalion personages of the Christmas Mumming Play. We have learnt to acknowledge the common origin of these two latter groups; may we not reasonably contemplate a possible relation existing between the two first named?

CHAPTER VIII

The Medicine Man

In previous chapters I have referred to the part played by the Doctor in a large number of the surviving 'Fertility' ceremonies, and to the fact, noted by other writers, that even where an active share is no longer assigned to the character, he still appears among the *dramatis personae* of these Folk-plays and processions.[1] We will now examine more closely the *rôle* allotted to this mysterious personage; we shall find it to be of extreme antiquity and remarkable significance.

In the interesting and important work by Professor von Schroeder, to which I have already often referred, we find the translation of a curious poem (*Rig-Veda*, 10.97), a monologue placed in the mouth of a Doctor, or Medicine Man, who vaunts the virtue of his herbs, and their power to cure human ills.[2] From the references made to a special sick man von Schroeder infers that this poem, like others in the collection, was intended to be acted, as well as recited, and that the personage to be healed, evidently present on the scene, was probably represented by a dummy, as no speeches are allotted to the character.

The entire poem consists of 23 verses of four lines each, and is divided by the translator into three distinct sections; the first is devoted to the praise of

[1] Cf. *supra*, Chap. 5, pp. 55, 57; Chap. 7, pp. 95, 96.
[2] *Mysterium und Mimus*, p. 369, *Der Mimus des Medizinmannes*.

herbs in general, their power to cure the sick man
before them, and at the same time to bring riches to
the Healer—the opening verses run:

> "The ancient herbs born long ago,
> Even three ages before the gods,
> Now the brown ones shall I praise!
> A hundred and seven kinds there are.
>
> A hundred kinds, my little mothers,
> A thousand branches do you have,
> With your strength a thousandfold,
> Heal and cure this man for me.
>
> Listen, you herbs, you little mothers,
> You divine ones, this I tell you,
> Horses, cattle and garments I want,
> And also to gain thy life, dear man!"

He then praises the power of all herbs:

> "From heaven did the hosts of herbs
> Come flying down and say to me,
> If we find him still alive,
> Free from harm this man shall be."

Finally the speaker singles out one herb as superior to all others:

> "In Soma's realm are many herbs,
> And knowledge a hundredfold have they,
> Of all these herbs thou art the best
> The wish to fulfil and heart to heal."

He conjures all other herbs to lend their virtue to
this special remedy:

> "All you herbs in Soma's kingdom,
> Over all the earth spread widely,
> Brihaspati's seed are you,
> Give to this herb all your strength!

May he who plants you know no harm,
Nor he for whom your seed is sown!
With us shall all, both man and beast,
Well and free from danger be.

All you who listen to my word,
You who are far away from here,
All you plants unite together,
And grant your strength to this one herb!"

And the herbs, taking counsel together with Soma
their king, answer:

"That man to whom a Brahman gives us,
Him shall we save from harm, O King."

a line which throws a light upon the personality of
the speaker; he is obviously a Brahmin, and the
Medicine Man here, as elsewhere, unites the functions of Priest and Healer.

Professor von Schroeder suggests that this Dramatic Monologue formed part of the ceremonies of
a Soma feast, that it is the Soma plant from which
the heavenly drink is brewed which is to be understood as the first of all herbs and the curer of all ills,
and the reference to Soma as King of the herbs seems
to bear out this suggestion.

In a previous chapter[3] I have referred to a curious
little poem, also found in the *Rig-Veda*, and translated by von Schroeder under the title *A Folk-Procession at a Soma-Feast*, the *dramatis personae* of the
poem offering, as I pointed out, a most striking and
significant parallel to certain surviving Fertility processions, notably that of Värdegötzen in Hanover.
In this little song which von Schroeder places in the
mouth of the leader of the band of maskers, the
Doctor is twice referred to; in the opening lines we
have the Brahmin, the Doctor, the Carpenter, the

[3] Cf. Chap. 5, pp. 56, 57.

Smith, given as men plying different trades, and each and all in search of gain; in the final verse the speaker announces, "I am a Poet (or Singer), my father a Doctor." Thus of the various trades and personages enumerated the Doctor alone appears twice over, an indication of the importance attached to this character.

Unfortunately, in view of the fragmentary condition of the survivals of early Aryan literature, and the lack of explanatory material at our disposal, it is impossible to decide what was the precise *rôle* assigned to the 'Medicine Man'; judging from the general character of the surviving dramatic fragments and the close parallel which exists between these fragments and the Medieval and Modern Fertility ceremonies, it seems extremely probable that his original *rôle* was identical with that assigned to his modern counterpart, *i.e.*, that of restoring to life or health the slain, or suffering, representative of the Vegetation Spirit.

This presumption gains additional support from the fact that it is in this character that the Doctor appears in Greek Classical Drama. Von Schroeder refers to the fact that the Doctor was a stock figure in the Greek 'Mimus'[4] and in Mr Cornford's interesting volume entitled *The Origin of Attic Comedy*, the author reckons the Doctor among the stock Masks of the early Greek Theatre, and assigns to this character the precise *rôle* which later survivals have led us to attribute to him.

The significance of Mr Cornford's work lies in the fact that, while he accepts Sir Gilbert Murray's deeply interesting and suggestive theory that the origins of Greek Tragedy are to be sought in "the Agon of the Fertility Spirit, his Pathos, and Theophany," he contends that a similar origin may be postu-

[4] *Op. cit.* p. 371.

lated for Attic Comedy—that the stock Masks (characters) agree with a theory of derivation of such Comedy from a ritual performance celebrating the renewal of the seasons.[5] "They were at first serious, and even awful, figures in a Religious Mystery, the God who every year is born, and dies, and rises again; his Mother and his Bride; the Antagonist who kills him; the Medicine Man who restores him to life."[6]

I would submit that the presence of such a character in the original ritual drama of Revival which, on my theory, underlies the romantic form of the Grail legend, may, in view of the above evidence, and of that brought forward in the previous chapters, be accepted as at least a probable hypothesis.

But, it may be objected, granting that the Doctor in these Fertility processions and dramas represents a genuine survival of a feature of immemorial antiquity, a survival to be traced alike in Aryan remains, in Greek literature, and in Medieval ceremony, what is the precise bearing upon the special subject of our investigations? There is no Doctor in the Grail legend, although there is certainly abundant scope for his activities!

There may be no Doctor in the Grail legend today, but was there never such a character? How if

[5] *Op. cit.* pp. 78 *et seq.*

[6] I would draw attention to the fact that while scholars are now coming to the conclusion that Classic Drama, whether Tragedy or Comedy, reposes for its origin upon this ancient ritual, others have pointed out that Modern Drama derives from the ritual Play of the Church, the first recorded medieval drama being the Easter *Quem Quaeritis?* the dramatic celebration of Our Lord's Resurrection. Cf. Chambers, *The Mediaeval Stage,* where this thesis is elaborately developed and illustrated. It is a curious fact that certain texts of this, the 'Classical' Passion Play, contain a scene between the Maries and the 'Unguentarius' from whom they purchase spices for the embalmment of Our Lord. Can this be a survival of the Medicine Man? (Cf. *op. cit.* Vol. II. p. 33.)

this be the key to explain the curious and persistent attribution of healing skill to so apparently unsuitable a personage as Sir Gawain? I would draw the attention of my readers to a passage in the *Perceval* of Chrétien de Troyes, where Gawain, finding a wounded knight by the roadside, proceeds to treat him:

> "Of wounds and healing lore
> Did Sir Gawain know more
> Than any man alive.
> To make the sick knight thrive,
> A herb to cure all pain
> That in a hedge had lain
> He spied, and thence he plucked it.[7]

Other MSS. are rather fuller:

> "Of wounds and healing lore
> Had Sir Gawain learned more
> Than any other knew.
> Within a hedge there grew
> A herb he long had known
> By his master he'd been shown
> And taught its healing spell,
> And so he knew it well.[8]

We find reference to Gawain's possession of medical knowledge elsewhere. In the poem entitled *Lancelot et le cerf au pied blanc*, Gawain, finding his friend desperately wounded, carries him to a physician whom he instructs as to the proper treatment.[9]

> "To the healer did Sir Gawain
> Teach his art of curing pain."[10]

In the parallel adventure related in *Morien Ga-*

[7] Bibl. Nat., fonds Français, 12577, fo. 40.
[8] Bibl. Nat., f. F. 1453, fo. 49. *Parzival*, Bk. x. ll. 413–22.
[9] *Lanceloet, Jonckbloet*, Vol. II. ll. 22271–23126.
[10] *Op. cit.* ll. 22825–26.

wain heals Lancelot without the aid of any physician:[11]

> "Then Sir Gawain was greatly pleased
> That by his herbs pain could be eased
> And Lancelot's bleeding wholly cured
> And healed the wounds he had endured."[12]

They ride to an anchorite's cell:

> "They went there with the single thought
> That at once the cure they sought
> Would by Sir Gawain be wrought."[13]

The Dutch *Lancelot* has numerous references to Gawain's skill in healing. Of course the advocates of the originality of Chrétien de Troyes will object that these references, though found in poems which have no connection with Chrétien, and which are translations from lost French originals of an undetermined date, are one and all loans from the more famous poem. This, however, can hardly be contended of the Welsh *Triads*; there we find Gwalchmai, the Welsh Gawain, cited as one of the three men "To whom the nature of every object was known,"[14] an accomplishment exceedingly necessary for a 'Medicine Man,' but not at first sight especially needful for the equipment of a knight.[15] This persistent attribution of healing skill is not, so far as my acquaintance with medieval Romance goes, paral-

[11] *Op. cit.* Vol. i. ll. 42540–47262.

[12] *Op. cit.* ll. 46671–74.

[13] *Op. cit.* ll. 46678–80.

[14] Cf. Loth, *Les Mabinogion*, Vol. ii. p. 230 and note. The other two are Riwallawn Walth Banhadlen, and Llacheu son of Arthur.

[15] The only instance in which I have found medicine directly connected with the knightly order is in the case of the warrior clan of the Samurai, in Japan, where members, physically unfitted for the task of a warrior, were trained as *Royal* Doctors, the *Folk* Doctors being recruited from a class below the Samurai. Cf. *Medizin der Natur-Völker*, Bartels, p. 65.

leled in the case of any other knight; even Tristan,
who is probably the most accomplished of heroes
of romance, the most thoroughly trained in all
branches of knightly education, is not credited with
any such knowledge. No other knight, save Gawain,
has the reputation of a Healer, yet Gawain, the
Maidens' Knight, the 'fair Father of Nurture' is, at
first sight, hardly the personage one might expect to
possess such skill. Why he should be so persistently
connected with healing was for long a problem to
me; recently, however, I have begun to suspect that
we have in this apparently motiveless attribution the
survival of an early stage of tradition in which not
only did Gawain cure the Grail King, but he did so,
not by means of a question, or by the welding of a
broken sword, but by more obvious and natural
means, the administration of a healing herb. Gawain's character of Healer belongs to him in his *rôle*
of Grail Winner.

Some years ago, in the course of my reading, I
came across a passage in which certain knights of
Arthur's court, riding through a forest, come upon a
herb 'which belonged to the Grail.' Unfortunately
the reference, at the time I met with it, though it
struck me as curious, did not possess any special
significance, and either I omitted to make a note of
it, or entered it in a book which, with sundry others,
went mysteriously astray in the process of moving
furniture. In any case, though I have searched dili-
gently I have failed to recover the passage, but I note
it here in the hope that one of my readers may be
more fortunate.

It is perhaps not without significance that a
mention of Peredur (Perceval) in Welsh poetry may
also possibly contain a reference to his healing office.
I refer to the well-known *Song of the Graves* in the
Black Book of Carmarthen where the grave of Mor,

son of Peredur Penwetic, is referred to. According to Dr G. Evans the word *penwedic,* or *perfeddyg,* as it may also be read, means *chief Healer.* Peredur, it is needless to say, is the Welsh equivalent of Perceval, Gawain's successor and supplanter in the *rôle* of Grail hero.

I have no desire to press the point unduly, but it is certainly significant that, entirely apart from any such theory of the evolution of the Grail legend as that advanced in these pages, a Welsh scholar should have suggested a rendering of the title of the Grail hero which is in complete harmony with that theory; a rendering also which places him side by side with his compatriot Gwalchmai, even as the completely evolved Grail story connects him with Gawain. In any case there is food for reflection in the fact that the possibility of such an origin once admitted, the most apparently incongruous, and inharmonious, elements of the story show themselves capable of a natural and unforced explanation.

In face of the evidence above set forth it seems impossible to deny that the Doctor, or Medicine Man, did, from the very earliest ages, play an important part in Dramatic Fertility Ritual, that he still survives in the modern Folk-play, the rude representative of the early ritual form, and it is at least possible that the attribution of healing skill to so romantic and chivalrous a character as Sir Gawain may depend upon the fact that, at an early, and pre-literary stage of his story, he played the *rôle* traditionally assigned to the Doctor, that of restoring to life and health the dead, or wounded, representative of the Spirit of Vegetation.

If I am right in my reading of this complicated problem the *mise-en-scène* of the Grail story was originally a loan from a ritual actually performed, and familiar to those who first told the tale. This ritual, in its earlier stages comparatively simple and objective in form, under the process of an insistence upon the inner and spiritual significance, took upon itself a more complex and esoteric character, the rite became a Mystery, and with this change the *rôle* of the principal actors became of heightened significance. That of the Healer could no longer be adequately fulfilled by the administration of a medicinal remedy; the relation of Body and Soul became of cardinal importance for the Drama, the Medicine Man gave place to the Redeemer; and his task involved more than the administration of the original Herbal remedy. In fact in the final development of the story the *Pathos* is shared alike by the representative of the Vegetation Spirit, and the Healer, whose task involves a period of stern testing and probation.

If we wish to understand clearly the evolution of the Grail story we must realize that the simple Fertility Drama from which it sprung has undergone a gradual and mysterious change, which has invested it with elements at once 'rich and strange,' and that though Folk-lore may be the key to unlock the outer portal of the Grail castle it will not suffice to give us the entrance to its deeper secrets.

APPENDIX TO CHAPTER VIII

While having no connection with the main subject of our study, the Grail legend, I should like to draw the attention of students of Medieval literature to the curious parallel between the *Rig-Veda* poem of the *Medicine Man* or *Kräuter-Lied* as it is also called, and Rustebœuf's *Dist de l'Erberie*. Both are monologues, both presuppose the presence of an audience, in each case the speaker is one who vaunts his skill in the use of herbs, in each case he has in view the ultimate gain to himself. Here are the opening lines of the Medieval poem:[1]

> "Welcome, my lords, both great and small,
> Young and old, you are welcome all,
> Pray do not think I would deceive,
> This fact you plainly can perceive
> As well as I; now sit down please,
> I shall not bore you, be at ease,
> I am a doctor."

He has been long with the lord of Caire, where he won much gold; in Puille, Calabre, Luserne.

> "These herbs I did gain
> Such great virtues contain
> That they cure every pain
> And put ills to flight."

There is no reference in the poem to a cure about to be performed in the presence of the audience, which does not however exclude the possibility of such cure being effected.

It would be interesting to know under what circumstances such a poem was recited, whether it formed part of a popular representation. The audience in view is of a mixed character, young and old, great and small, and one has a vision of the Quack Doctor at some village fair, on the platform before his booth, declaiming the virtues of his nostrums before an audience representative of all ranks and ages. It is a far cry from such a Medieval scene to the prehistoric days of the *Rig-Veda*, but the *mise-en-scène* is the same; the popular 'seasonal' feast, the Doctor with his healing herbs, which he vaunts in skilful rhyme, the hearers, drawn from all ranks, some credulous, some amused. There

[1] Cf. *Œuvres de Rutebœuf*, Kressner, p. 115.

seems very little doubt that both poems are specimens, and very good specimens, of a *genre* the
popularity and vitality of which are commensurate
with the antiquity of its origin.[2]

[2] My attention was drawn to the poem by references to it
in *The Mediaeval Stage,* Chambers.

CHAPTER IX

The Fisher King

THE gradual process of our investigation has led us to the conclusion that the elements forming the existing Grail legend—the setting of the story, the nature of the task which awaits the hero, the symbols and their significance—one and all, while finding their counterpart in prehistoric record, present remarkable parallels to the extant practice and belief of countries so widely separate as the British Isles, Russia, and Central Africa.

The explanation of so curious a fact, for it is a fact, and not a mere hypothesis, may, it was suggested, most probably be found in the theory that in this fascinating literature we have the, sometimes partially understood, sometimes wholly misinterpreted, record of a ritual, originally presumed to exercise a life-giving potency, which, at one time of universal observance, has, even in its decay, shown itself possessed of elements of the most persistent vitality.

That if the ritual, which according to our theory lies at the root of the Grail story, be indeed the ritual of a Life Cult, it should, in and per se, possess precisely these characteristics, will, I think, be admitted by any fair-minded critic; the point of course is, can we definitely prove our theory, i.e., not merely point to striking parallels, but select, from the figures and incidents composing our story, some one element, which, by showing itself capable of explanation on this theory, and on this theory alone, may be held to afford decisive proof of the soundness of our hypothesis?

It seems to me that there is one such element in the bewildering complex, by which the theory can be thus definitely tested, that is the personality of the central figure and the title by which he is known. If we can prove that the Fisher King, *qua* Fisher King, is an integral part of the ritual, and can be satisfactorily explained alike by its intention, and inherent symbolism, we shall, I think, have taken the final step which will establish our theory upon a sure basis. On the other hand, if the Fisher King, *qua* Fisher King, does not fit into our framework we shall be forced to conclude that, while the *provenance* of certain elements of the Grail literature is practically assured, the *ensemble* has been complicated by the introduction of a terminology, which, whether the outcome of serious intention, or of mere literary caprice, was foreign to the original source, and so far, defies explanation. In this latter case our theory would not necessarily be *manqué*, but would certainly be seriously incomplete.

We have already seen that the personality of the King, the nature of the disability under which he is suffering, and the reflex effect exercised upon his folk and his land, correspond, in a most striking manner, to the intimate relation at one time held to exist between the ruler and his land; a relation mainly dependent upon the identification of the King with the Divine principle of Life and Fertility.

This relation, as we have seen above, exists today among certain African tribes.

If we examine more closely into the existing variants of our romances, we shall find that those very variants are not only thoroughly *dans le cadre* of our proposed solution, but also afford a valuable, and hitherto unsuspected, indication of the relative priority of the versions.

In Chapter 1, I discussed the task of the hero in general, here I propose to focus attention upon his host, and while in a measure traversing the same ground, to do so with a view to determining the true character of this enigmatic personage.

In the *Bleheris* version,[1] the lord of the castle is suffering under no disability whatever; he is described as "tall, and strong of limb, of no great age, but somewhat bald." Besides the King there is a Dead Knight upon a bier, over whose body Vespers for the Dead are solemnly sung. The wasting of the land, partially restored by Gawain's question concerning the Lance, has been caused by the 'Dolorous Stroke,' *i.e.*, the stroke which brought about the death of the Knight, whose identity is here never revealed. Certain versions which interpolate the account of Joseph of Arimathea and the Grail, allude to 'Le riche Pescheur' and his heirs as Joseph's descendants, and, presumably, for it is not directly stated, guardians of the Grail,[2] but the King himself is here never called by that title. From his connection with the Waste Land it seems more probable that it was the Dead Knight who filled that *rôle*.

In the second version of which Gawain is the hero, that of *Diû Crône*,[3] the Host is an old and infirm man. After Gawain has asked the question we learn that he is really dead, and only compelled to retain the semblance of life till the task of the

[1] Cf. my *Sir Gawain at the Grail Castle*, pp. 3–30. The best text is that of MS. B.N., fonds Franç. 12576, ff. 87*vo*–91. The above remarks apply also to the *Elucidation*, which is using a version of the *Bleheris* form.

[2] B.N. 12577, fo. 136*vo*.

[3] Cf. *Sir Gawain at the Grail Castle*, pp. 33–46.

Quester be achieved. Here, again, he is not called the Fisher King.

In the *Perceval* versions, on the contrary, we find the name invariably associated with him, but he is not always directly connected with the misfortunes which have fallen upon his land. Thus, while the Wauchier texts are incomplete, breaking off at the critical moment of asking the question, Manessier who continues, and ostensibly completes, Wauchier, introduces the Dead Knight, here Goondesert, or Gondefer (which I suspect is the more correct form), brother of the King, whose death by treachery has plunged the land in misery, and been the direct cause of the self-wounding of the King.[4] The healing of the King and the restoration of the land depend upon Perceval's slaying the murderer Partinal. These two versions show a combination of Perceval and Gawain themes, such as their respective dates might lead us to expect.

Robert de Borron is the only writer who gives a clear, and tolerably reasonable, account of why the guardian of the Grail bears the title of Fisher King; in other cases, such as the poems of Chrétien and Wolfram, the name is connected with his partiality for fishing, an obviously *post hoc* addition.

The story in question is found in Borron's *Joseph of Arimathea*.[5] Here we are told how, during the wanderings of that holy man and his companions in the wilderness, certain of the company fell into sin. By the command of God, Brons, Joseph's brother-in-law, caught a Fish, which, with the Grail, provided a mystic meal of which the unworthy cannot partake; thus the sinners were separated from the righteous. Henceforward Brons was known as 'The Rich Fisher.' It is noteworthy, however, that

---

[4] Cf. B.N. 12576, ff. 220–222vo and fo. 258.
[5] Hucher, *Le Saint Graal*, Vol. I. pp. 251 *et seq.*, 315 *et seq.*

in the Perceval romance, ascribed to Borron, the title is as a rule, *Roi* Pescheur, not *Riche* Pescheur.[6]

In this romance the King is not suffering from any special malady, but is the victim of extreme old age; not surprising, as he is Brons himself, who has survived from the dawn of Christianity to the days of King Arthur. We are told that the effect of asking the question will be to restore him to youth;[7] as a matter of fact it appears to bring about his death, as he only lives three days after his restoration.[8]

When we come to Chrétien's poem we find ourselves confronted with a striking alteration in the presentment. There are, not one, but two, disabled kings; one suffering from the effects of a wound, the other in extreme old age. Chrétien's poem being incomplete we do not know what he intended to be the result of the achieved Quest, but we may I think reasonably conclude that the wounded King at least was healed.[9]

The *Parzival* of von Eschenbach follows the same tradition, but is happily complete. Here we find the wounded King was healed, but what becomes of the aged man (here the grandfather, not as in Chrétien the father, of the Fisher King) we are not told.[10]

The *Perlesvaus* is, as I have noted above,[11] very

6 Cf. Modena MS. pp. 11, 12, 21, etc.; Dr Nitze, *The Fisher-King in the Grail Romances*, p. 373, says Borron uses the term *Rice* Pescheur, as opposed to the *Roi* Pescheur of Chrétien. This remark is only correct as applied to the *Joseph*.

7 Modena MS. p. 61 and note.

8 *Ibid.* p. 63.

9 The evidence of the *Parzival* and the parallel Grail sections of *Sone de Nansai*, which appear to repose ultimately on a source common to all three authors, makes this practically certain.

10 This is surely a curious omission, if the second King were as essential a part of the scheme as Dr Nitze supposes.

11 Cf. Chapter 2, p. 16

unsatisfactory. The illness of the King is badly
motived, and he dies before the achievement of
the Quest. This romance, while retaining certain
interesting, and undoubtedly primitive features,
is, as a whole, too late, and *remaniée* a redaction
to be of much use in determining the question of
origins.

The same may be said of the *Grand Saint Graal*
and *Queste* versions, both of which are too closely
connected with the prose *Lancelot,* and too obviously intended to develope and complete the
données of that romance to be relied upon as evidence for the original form of the Grail legend.[12]
The version of the *Queste* is very confused: there
are two kings at the Grail castle, Pelles, and his
father; sometimes the one, sometimes the other,
bears the title of Roi Pescheur.[13] There is besides,
an extremely old, and desperately wounded, king,
Mordrains, a contemporary of Joseph, who practically belongs, not to the Grail tradition, but to a
Conversion legend embodied in the *Grand Saint
Graal.*[14] Finally, in the latest cyclic texts, we have
three Kings, all of whom are wounded.[15]

The above will show that the presentment of
this central figure is much confused; generally

[12] I cannot agree with Dr Nitze's remark (*op. cit.* p. 374)
that "in most versions the Fisher King has a mysterious double." I hold the feature to be a peculiarity of the Chrétien-
Wolfram group. It is not found in the Gawain versions, in
Wauchier, nor in Manessier. Gerbert is using the *Queste* in
the passage relative to Mordrains, and for the reason stated
above I hold that neither *Queste* nor *Grand Saint Graal* should
be cited when we are dealing, as Dr Nitze is here dealing,
with questions of ultimate origin.

[13] Cf. my *Legend of Sir Lancelot,* pp. 167 and 168.

[14] Cf. Heinzel, *Ueber die Alt-Franz. Gral-Romanen,* pp.
136 and 137.

[15] Cf. *Legend of Sir Perceval,* Vol. ii. p. 343, note. These
three kings are found in the curious *Merlin* MS. B.N., f. Franç.
337, fo. 249 *et seq.*

termed Le Roi Pescheur, he is sometimes described as in middle life, and in full possession of his bodily powers. Sometimes while still comparatively young he is incapacitated by the effects of a wound, and is known also by the title of Roi Mehaigné, or Maimed King. Sometimes he is in extreme old age, and in certain closely connected versions the two ideas are combined, and we have a wounded Fisher King, and an aged father, or grandfather. But I would draw attention to the significant fact that in no case is the Fisher King a youthful character; that distinction is reserved for his Healer, and successor.

Now is it possible to arrive at any conclusion as to the relative value and probable order of these conflicting variants? I think that if we admit that they do, in all probability, represent a more or less coherent survival of the Nature ritual previously discussed, we may, by help of what we know as to the varying forms of that ritual, be enabled to bring some order out of this confusion.

If we turn back to Chapters 4, 5, and 7, and consult the evidence there given as to the Adonis cults, the Spring Festivals of European Folk, the Mumming Plays of the British Isles, the main fact that emerges is that in the great majority of these cases the representative of the Spirit of Vegetation is considered as dead, and the object of these ceremonies is to restore him to life. This I hold to be the primary form.

This section had already been written when I came across the important article by Dr Jevons, referred to in a previous chapter.[16] Certain of his remarks are here so much to the point that I cannot refrain from quoting them. Speaking of the Mumming Plays, the writer says: "The one point in which

[16] *Vide supra*, pp. 96, 97.

there is no variation is that—the character is killed and brought to life again. The play is a ceremonial performance, or rather it is the development in dramatic form of what was originally a religious or magical rite, representing or realizing the revivification of the character slain. This revivification is the one essential and invariable feature of all the Mummer's plays in England."[17]

In certain cases, *e.g.*, the famous Roman Spring festival of Mamurius Veturius and the Swabian ceremony referred to above,[18] the central figure is an old man. In no case do I find that the representative of Vegetation is merely wounded, although the nature of the ritual would obviously admit of such a variant.

Thus, taking the extant and recognized forms of the ritual into consideration, we might expect to find that in the earliest, and least contaminated, version of the Grail story the central figure would be dead, and the task of the Quester that of restoring him to life. Viewed from this standpoint the *Gawain* versions (the priority of which is maintainable upon strictly literary grounds, Gawain being the original Arthurian romantic hero) are of extraordinary interest. In the one form we find a Dead Knight, whose fate is distinctly stated to have involved his land in desolation, in the other, an aged man who, while preserving the semblance of life, is in reality dead.

This last version appears to me, in view of our present knowledge, to be of extreme critical value. There can, I think, be little doubt that in the primary form underlying our extant versions the King was dead, and restored to life; at first, I strongly suspect, by the agency of some mysterious

17 *Op. cit.* p. 184.
18 Cf. Chapter 5, p. 55, Chap. 7, p. 92.

herb, or herbs, a feature retained in certain forms of the Mumming play.

In the next stage, that represented by Borron, he is suffering from extreme old age, and the task of the Quester is to restore him to youth. This version is again supported by extant parallels. In each of these cases it seems most probable that the original ritual (I should wish it to be clearly understood that I hold the Grail story to have been primarily dramatic, and actually performed) involved an act of substitution. The Dead King in the first case being probably represented by a mere effigy, in the second being an old man, his place was, at a given moment of the ritual, taken by the youth who played the *rôle* of the Quester. It is noteworthy that, while both Perceval and Galahad are represented as mere lads, Gawain, whatever his age at the moment of the Grail quest, was, as we learn from *Diû Crône*, dowered by his fairy Mistress with the gift of eternal youth.[19]

The versions of Chrétien and Wolfram, which present us with a wounded Fisher King, and a father, or grandfather,[20] in extreme old age, are due in my opinion to a literary device, intended to combine two existing variants. That the subject matter was well understood by the original redactor of the common source is proved by the nature of the injury,[21] but I hold that in these versions we have passed from the domain of ritual to that of literature. Still, we have a curious indication that the Wounding variant may have had its place in the former. The suggestion made above as to the probable existence in the primitive ritual

[19] *Diû Crône*, ll. 17329 *et seq.*

[20] In the *Parzival* Titurel is grandfather to Anfortas, Frimutel intervening; critics of the poem are apt to overlook this difference between the German and French versions.

[21] Cf. Chapter 2, p. 22.

of a substitution ceremony, seems to me to provide
a possible explanation of the feature found alike in
Wolfram, and in the closely allied Grail section of
Sone de Nansai; i.e., that the wound of the King
was a punishment for sin, he had conceived a passion
for a Pagan princess.[22] Now there would be no
incongruity in representing the Dead King as reborn
in youthful form, the aged King as "restored to
youth," but when the central figure was a man in the
prime of life some reason had to be found, his
strength and vitality being restored, for his supersession by the appointed Healer. This supersession
was adequately motived by the supposed trans-
gression of a fundamental Christian law, entailing
as consequence the forfeiture of his crown.

I would thus separate the *doubling* theme, as
found in Chrétien and Wolfram, from the *wounded*
theme, equally common to these poets. This latter
might possibly be accounted for on the ground of
a ritual variant; the first is purely literary, explicable
neither on the exoteric, nor the esoteric, aspect
of the ceremony. From the exoteric point of view
there are not, and there cannot be, two Kings suffering from parallel disability; the ritual knows one
Principle of Life, and one alone. Equally from the
esoteric standpoint Fisher King, and Maimed King,
representing two different aspects of the same
personality, may, and probably were, represented
as two individuals, but one alone is disabled. Further, as the two are, in very truth, one, they should
be equals in age, not of different generations. Thus
the *Bleheris* version which gives us a Dead Knight,
presumably, from his having been slain in battle,
still in vigorous manhood, and a hale King is,
ritually, the more correct. The original of Manessier's

[22] Cf. here my notes on *Sone de Nansai* (*Romania,* Vol.
XLIII. p. 412).

version must have been similar, but the fact that by the time it was compiled the Fisher King was generally accepted as being also the Maimed King led to the introduction of the very awkward, and poorly motived, self-wounding incident. It will be noted that in this case the King is not healed either at the moment of the slaying of his brother's murderer (which would be the logical result of the *données* of the tale), nor at the moment of contact with the successful Quester, but at the mere announcement of his approach.[23]

Thus, if we consider the King, apart from his title, we find that alike from his position in the story, his close connection with the fortunes of his land and people, and the varying forms of the disability of which he is the victim, he corresponds with remarkable exactitude to the central figure of a well-recognized Nature ritual, and may therefore justly be claimed to belong *ab origine* to such a hypothetical source.

But what about his title, why should he be called the *Fisher* King?

Here we strike what I hold to be the main *crux* of the problem, a feature upon which scholars have expended much thought and ingenuity, a feature which the authors of the romances themselves either did not always understand, or were at pains to obscure by the introduction of the obviously *post hoc* "motif" above referred to, *i.e.*, that he was called the Fisher King because of his devotion to the pastime of fishing: *à-propos* of which Heinzel sensibly re-

---

[23] In connection with my previous remarks on the subject (p. 119) I would point out that the *Queste* and *Grand Saint Graal* versions repeat the Maimed King *motif* in the most unintelligent manner. The element of old age, inherent in the Evalach-Mordrains incident, is complicated and practically obscured, by an absurdly exaggerated wounding element, here devoid of its original significance.

marks, that the story of the Fisher King "presupposes a legend of this personage only vaguely known and remembered by Chrétien."[24]

Practically the interpretations already attempted fall into two main groups, which we may designate as the Christian-Legendary, and the Celtic-Folk-lore interpretations. For those who hold that the Grail story is essentially, and fundamentally, Christian, finding its root in Eucharistic symbolism, the title is naturally connected with the use of the Fish symbol in early Christianity: the *Icthys* anagram, as applied to Christ, the title 'Fishers of Men,' bestowed upon the Apostles, the Papal ring of the Fisherman—though it must be noted that no manipulation of the Christian symbolism avails satisfactorily to account for the lamentable condition into which the bearer of the title has fallen.[25]

The advocates of the Folk-lore theory, on the other hand, practically evade this main difficulty, by basing their interpretation upon Borron's story of the catching of the Fish by Brons, equating this character with the Bran of Welsh tradition, and pointing to the existence, in Irish and Welsh legend, of a Salmon of Wisdom, the tasting of whose flesh confers all knowledge. Hertz acutely remarks that the incident, as related by Borron, is not of such importance as to justify the stress laid upon the

[24] Heinzel, *op. cit.* p. 13.

[25] For an instance of the extravagances to which a strictly Christian interpretation can lead, cf. Dr Sebastian Evans's theories set forth in his translation of the *Perlesvaus* (*The High History of the Holy Grail*) and in his *The Quest of the Holy Grail*. The author places the origin of the cycle in the first quarter of the thirteenth century, and treats it as an allegory of the position in England during the Interdict pronounced against King John, and the consequent withholding of the Sacraments. His identification of the characters with historical originals is most ingenious, an extraordinary example of misapplied learning.

name, Rich Fisher, by later writers.[26] We may also note in this connection that the Grail romances never employ the form 'Wise Fisher,' which, if the origin of the name were that proposed above, we might reasonably expect to find. It is obvious that a satisfactory solution of the problem must be sought elsewhere.

In my opinion the key to the puzzle is to be found in the rightful understanding of the *Fish-Fisher* symbolism. Students of the Grail literature have been too prone to treat the question on the Christian basis alone, oblivious of the fact that Christianity did no more than take over, and adapt to its own use, a symbolism already endowed with a deeply rooted prestige and importance.

So far the subject cannot be said to have received adequate treatment; certain of its aspects have been more or less fully discussed in monographs and isolated articles, but we still await a comprehensive study on this most important question.[27]

So far as the present state of our knowledge goes we can affirm with certainty that the Fish is a Life symbol of immemorial antiquity, and that the title of Fisher has, from the earliest ages, been associated with Deities who were held to be specially connected with the origin and preservation of Life.

[26] For a general discussion of the conflicting views cf. Dr Nitze's study, referred to above. The writer devotes special attention to the works of the late Prof. Heinzel and Mr Alfred Nutt as leading representatives of their respective schools.

[27] R. Pischel's *Ueber die Ursprung des Christlichen Fisch-Symbols* is specially devoted to the possible derivation from Indian sources. Scheftelowitz, *Das Fischsymbolik in Judentum und Christentum* (*Archiv für Religionswissenschaft*, Vol. XIV.), contains a great deal of valuable material. R. Eisler, *Orpheus the Fisher* (*The Quest*, Vols. I. and II.), *John, Jonas, Joannes* (*ibid.* Vol. III.), *The Messianic Fish-meal of the Primitive Church* (*ibid.* Vol. IV.), are isolated studies, forming part of a comprehensive work on the subject, the publication of which has unfortunately been prevented by the War.

In Indian cosmogony Manu finds a little fish in the water in which he would wash his hands; it asks, and receives, his protection, asserting that when grown to full size it will save Manu from the universal deluge. This is Jhasa, the greatest of all fish.[28]

The first Avatar of Vishnu the Creator is a Fish. At the great feast in honour of this god, held on the twelfth day of the first month of the Indian year, Vishnu is represented under the form of a golden Fish, and addressed in the following terms: "As Thou, O God, hast in the form of a fish saved the Vedas who were in the underworld, save me also."[29] The Fish Avatar was afterwards transferred to Buddha.

In Buddhist religion the symbols of the Fish and Fisher are freely employed. Thus in Buddhist monasteries we find drums and gongs in the shape of a fish, but the true meaning of the symbol, while still regarded as sacred, has been lost, and the explanations, like the explanations of the Grail romances, are often fantastic afterthoughts.

In the Māhāyana scriptures Buddha is referred to as the Fisherman who draws fish from the ocean of Samsara to the light of Salvation. There are figures and pictures which represent Buddha in the act of fishing, an attitude which, unless interpreted in a symbolic sense, would be utterly at variance with the tenets of the Buddhist religion.[30]

This also holds good for Chinese Buddhism. The goddess Kwanyin (=Avalokiteśvara), the female Deity of Mercy and Salvation, is depicted either on, or holding, a Fish. In the Han palace of Kun-

[28] *Mahâbhârata*, Bk. III.

[29] Cf. Scheftelowitz, *op. cit.* p. 51.

[30] Cf. *The Open Court*, June and July, 1911, where reproductions of these figures will be found.

Ming-Ch'ih there was a Fish carved in jade to which in time of drought sacrifices were offered, the prayers being always answered.

Both in India and China the Fish is employed in funeral rites. In India a crystal bowl with Fish handles was found in a reputed tomb of Buddha. In China the symbol is found on stone slabs enclosing the coffin, on bronze urns, vases, etc. Even as the Babylonians had the Fish, or Fisher, god, Oannes who revealed to them the arts of Writing, Agriculture, etc., and was, as Eisler puts it, 'teacher and lord of all wisdom,' so the Chinese Fu-Hi, who is pictured with the mystic tablets containing the mysteries of Heaven and Earth, is, with his consort and retinue, represented as having a fish's tail.[31]

The writer of the article in *The Open Court* asserts that "the Fish was sacred to those deities who were supposed to lead men back from the shadows of death to life."[32] If this be really the case we can understand the connection of the symbol first with Orpheus, later with Christ, as Eisler remarks: "Orpheus is connected with nearly all the mystery, and a great many of the ordinary chthonic, cults in Greece and Italy. Christianity took its first tentative steps into the reluctant world of Graeco-Roman Paganism under the benevolent patronage of Orpheus."[33]

There is thus little reason to doubt that, if we regard the Fish as a Divine Life symbol, of immemorial antiquity, we shall not go very far astray.

We may note here that there was a fish known to

[31] *Op. cit.* p. 403. Cf. here an illustration in Miss Harrison's *Themis* (p. 262), which shows Cecrops, who played the same *rôle* with regard to the Greeks, with a serpent's tail.

[32] *Ibid.* p. 168. In this connection note the prayer to Vishnu, quoted above.

[33] Cf. Eisler, *Orpheus the Fisher* (*The Quest*, Vol. 1. p. 126).

the Semites by the name of Adonis, although as
the title signifies 'Lord,' and is generic rather than
specific, too much stress cannot be laid upon it.
It is more interesting to know that in Babylonian
cosmology Adapa the Wise, the son of Ea, is
represented as a Fisher.[34] In the ancient Sumerian
laments for Tammuz, previously referred to, that
god is frequently addressed as *Divine Lamgar,
Lord of the Net,* the nearest equivalent I have so far
found to our 'Fisher King.'[35] Whether the phrase
is here used in an actual or a symbolic sense the
connection of idea is sufficiently striking.

In the opinion of the most recent writers on the
subject the Christian Fish symbolism derives directly
from the Jewish, the Jews, on their side having
borrowed freely from Syrian belief and practice.[36]

What may be regarded as the central point of
Jewish Fish symbolism is the tradition that, at the
end of the world, Messias will catch the great Fish
Leviathan, and divide its flesh as food among the
faithful. As a foreshadowing of this Messianic Feast
the Jews were in the habit of eating fish upon the
Sabbath. During the Captivity, under the influence
of the worship of the goddess Atargatis, they transferred the ceremony to the Friday, the eve of the
Sabbath, a position which it has retained to the
present day. Eisler remarks that "in Galicia one can
see Israelite families in spite of their being reduced

[34] Cf. W. Staerk, *Ueber den Ursprung der Gral-Legende,*
pp. 55, 56.
[35] Cf. S. Langdon, *Sumerian and Babylonian Psalms,* pp.
301, 305, 307, 313.
[36] Cf. Eisler, *The Messianic Fish-meal of the Primitive
Church* (*The Quest,* Vol. iv.), where the various frescoes are
described; also the article by Scheftelowitz, already referred
to. While mainly devoted to Jewish beliefs and practices, this
study contains much material derived from other sources. So
far it is the fullest and most thoroughly *documenté* treatment
of the subject I have met with.

to the extremest misery, procuring on Fridays a single gudgeon, to eat, divided into fragments, at night-fall. In the 16th century Rabbi Solomon Luria protested strongly against this practice. Fish, he declared, should be eaten on the Sabbath itself, not on the Eve."[37]

This Jewish custom appears to have been adopted by the primitive Church, and early Christians, on their side, celebrated a Sacramental Fish-meal. The Catacombs supply us with numerous illustrations, fully described by the two writers referred to. The elements of this mystic meal were Fish, Bread, and Wine, the last being represented in the Messianic tradition: "At the end of the meal God will give to the most worthy, *i.e.*, to King David, the Cup of Blessing—one of fabulous dimensions."[38]

Fish play an important part in Mystery Cults, as being the 'holy' food. Upon a tablet dedicated to the Phrygian *Magna Mater* we find Fish and Cup; and Dölger, speaking of a votive tablet discovered in the Balkans, says, "Here the fish always stands out very clearly as the holy food of a Mystery Cult."[39]

Now I would submit that here, and not in Celtic Folk-lore, is to be found the source of Borron's Fish-meal. Let us consider the circumstances. Joseph and his followers, in the course of their wanderings, find themselves in danger of famine. The position is somewhat curious, as apparently the leaders have no idea of the condition of their followers till the latter appeal to Brons.[40]

Brons informs Joseph, who prays for aid and counsel from the Grail. A Voice from Heaven bids

[37] Cf. Eisler, *op. cit.* and Scheftelowitz, pp. 19, 20.
[38] Cf. Eisler, *op. cit.* p. 508.
[39] Cf. Scheftelowitz, *op. cit.* pp. 337, 338 and note 4.
[40] Hucher, *Le Saint Graal*, Vol. I. pp. 251 *et seq.*, 315 *et seq.*

him send his brother-in-law, Brons, to catch a fish. Meanwhile he, Joseph, is to prepare a table, set the Grail, covered with a cloth, in the centre opposite his own seat, and the fish which Brons shall catch, on the other side. He does this, and the seats are filled—"A great many were seated there, and there were more of those who did not sit at all than of those who did." Those who are seated at the table are conscious of a great "douceur," and "contentment of their hearts," the rest feel nothing.

Now compare this with the Irish story of the Salmon of Wisdom.[41]

Finn Mac Cumhail enters the service of his name-sake, Finn Eger, who for seven years had remained by the Boyne watching the Salmon of Lynn Feic, which it had been foretold Finn should catch. The younger lad, who conceals his name, catches the fish. He is set to watch it while it roasts but is warned not to eat it. Touching it with his thumb he is burned, and puts his thumb in his mouth to cool it. Immediately he becomes possessed of all knowl-edge, and thereafter has only to chew his thumb to obtain wisdom. Mr Nutt remarks: "The incident in Borron's poem has been recast in the mould of mediaeval Christian Symbolism, but I think the older myth can still be clearly discerned, and is wholly responsible for the incident as found in the *Conte du Graal.*"

But when these words were written we were in ignorance of the Sacramental Fish-meal, common alike to Jewish, Christian, and Mystery Cults, a meal which offers a far closer parallel to Borron's romance than does the Finn story, in which, beyond the catching of a fish, there is absolutely no point of contact with our romance, neither Joseph nor

[41] Cf. A. Nutt, *Studies in the Legend of the Holy Grail*, p. 209.

Brons derives wisdom from the eating thereof; it
is not they who detect the sinners, the severance
between the good and the evil is brought about
automatically. The Finn story has no common meal,
and no idea of spiritual blessings such as are connected therewith.

In the case of the Messianic Fish-meal, on the
other hand, the parallel is striking; in both cases it
is a communal meal, in both cases the privilege
of sharing it is the reward of the faithful, in both
cases it is a foretaste of the bliss of Paradise.

Furthermore, as remarked above, the practice
was at one time of very widespread prevalence.

Now whence did Borron derive his knowledge,
from Jewish, Christian or Mystery sources?

This is a question not very easy to decide. In
view of the pronounced Christian tone of Borron's
romance I should feel inclined to exclude the first,
also the Jewish Fish-meal seems to have been of a
more open, general and less symbolic character than
the Christian; it was frankly an anticipation of a
promised future bliss, obtainable by all.

Orthodox Christianity, on the other hand, knows
nothing of a Sacred Fish-meal, so far as I am aware
it forms no part of any Apocalyptic expectation,
and where this special symbolism does occur it is
often under conditions which place its interpretation
outside the recognized category of Christian belief.

A noted instance in point is the famous epitaph of
Bishop Aberkios, over the correct interpretation of
which scholars have spent much time and ingenuity.[42] In this curious text Aberkios, after mention-
ing his journeys, says:

"Paul I had as my guide,

[42] Cf. Eisler, *The Mystic Epitaph of Bishop Aberkios* (*The
Quest*, Vol. v. pp. 302–312); Scheftelowitz, *op. cit.* p. 8.

Faith however always went ahead and set before me
    as food a *Fish* from a *Fountain,* a huge one, a
    clean one,
Which a *Holy Virgin* has *caught.*
This she gave to the friends ever to eat as food,
Having good *Wine,* and offering it watered together
    with *Bread.*
Aberkios had this engraved when 72 years of age in
    truth.
Whoever can understand this let him pray for
    Aberkios."

Eisler (I am here quoting from the *Quest* article)
remarks, "As the last line of our quotation gives us
quite plainly to understand, a number of words
which we have italicized are obviously used in an
unusual, metaphorical, sense, that is to say as terms
of the Christian Mystery language." While Harnack,
admitting that the Christian character of the text
is indisputable, adds significantly: "But it is not the
Christianity of the Church."

Thus it is possible that, to the various points of
doubtful orthodoxy which scholars have noted as
characteristic of the Grail romances, Borron's Fish-
meal should also be added.

Should it be objected that the dependence of a
medieval romance upon a Jewish tradition of such
antiquity is scarcely probable, I would draw attention to the *Voyage of Saint Brandan,* where the
monks, during their prolonged wanderings, annually
'kept their Resurrection,' *i.e.,* celebrate their Easter
Mass, on the back of a great Fish.[43] On their first
meeting with this monster Saint Brandan tells them
it is the greatest of all fishes, and is named Jastoni,
a name which bears a curious resemblance to the

[43] Cf. *The Voyage of Saint Brandan,* ll. 372 *et seq.,* 660
et seq.

Jhasa of the Indian tradition cited above.[44] In this last instance the connection of the Fish with life, renewed and sustained, is undeniable.

The original source of such a symbol is most probably to be found in the belief, referred to in a previous chapter,[45] that all life comes from the water, but that a more sensual and less abstract idea was also operative appears from the close connection of the Fish with the goddess Astarte or Atargatis, a connection here shared by the Dove. Cumont, in his *Les Religions Orientales dans le Paganisme Romain,* says: "Two animals were held in general reverence, namely, Dove and Fish. Countless flocks of Doves greeted the traveller when he stepped on shore at Askalon, and in the outer courts of all the temples of Astarte one might see the flutter of their white wings. The Fish were preserved in ponds near to the Temple, and superstitious dread forbade their capture, for the goddess punished such sacrilege, smiting the offender with ulcers and tumours."[46]

But at certain mystic banquets priests and initiates partook of this otherwise forbidden food, in the belief that they thus partook of the flesh of the goddess. Eisler and other scholars are of opinion that it was the familiarity with this ritual gained by the Jews during the Captivity that led to the adoption of the Friday Fish-meal, already referred to, Friday being the day dedicated to the goddess and, later, to her equivalent, Venus. From the Jews the custom spread to the Christian Church, where it still flourishes, its true origin, it is needless to say, being wholly unsuspected.[47]

[44] *Op. cit.* ll. 170 *et seq.,* and *supra,* p. 126.
[45] *Vide supra,* p. 74.
[46] *Op. cit.* p. 168.
[47] Cf. *The Messianic Fish-meal.*

Dove and Fish also appear together in ancient iconography. In Comte Goblet d'Alviella's work *The Migration of Symbols* there is an illustration of a coin of Cyzicus, on which is represented an Omphalus, flanked by two Doves, with a Fish beneath;[48] and a whole section is devoted to the discussion of the representations of two Doves on either side of a Temple entrance, or of an Omphalus. In the author's opinion the origin of the symbol may be found in the sacred dove-cotes of Phoenicia, referred to by Cumont.

Scheftelowitz instances the combination of Fish-meal and Dove, found on a Jewish tomb of the first century at Syracuse, and remarks that the two are frequently found in combination on Christian tomb-stones.[49]

Students of the Grail romances will not need to be reminded that the Dove makes its appearance in certain of our texts. In the *Parzival* it plays a some-what important *rôle;* every Good Friday a Dove brings from Heaven a Host, which it lays upon the Grail; and the Dove is the badge of the Grail Knights.[50] In the prose *Lancelot* the coming of the Grail procession is heralded by the entrance through the window of a Dove, bearing a censer in its beak.[51] Is it not possible that it was the already existing con-nection in Nature ritual of these two, Dove and Fish, which led to the introduction of the former into our romances, where its *rôle* is never really adequately motived? It is further to be noted that besides Dove and Fish the Syrians reverenced Stones, more espe-cially meteoric Stones, which they held to be en-

[48] *Op. cit.* p. 92, fig. 42 *a.*
[49] *Op. cit.* p. 23, and note, p. 29.
[50] *Parzival,* Bk. ix. ll. 1109 *et seq.,* Bk. xvi. ll. 175 *et seq.*
[51] Cf. *Sir Gawain at the Grail Castle,* p. 55. Certain of the *Lancelot* MSS., *e.g.,* B.N., f. Fr. 123, give two doves.

dowed with life potency, another point of contact with our romances.[52]

That the Fish was considered a potent factor in ensuring fruitfulness is proved by certain prehistoric tablets described by Scheftelowitz, where Fish, Horse, and Swastika, or in another instance Fish and Reindeer, are found in a combination which unmistakeably denotes that the object of the votive tablet was to ensure the fruitfulness of flocks and herds.[53]

With this intention its influence was also invoked in marriage ceremonies. The same writer points out that the Jews in Poland were accustomed to hold a Fish feast immediately on the conclusion of the marriage ceremony and that a similar practice can be proved for the ancient Greeks.[54] At the present day the Jews of Tunis exhibit a Fish's tail on a cushion at their weddings.[55] In some parts of India the newly-wedded pair waded knee-deep into the water, and caught fish in a new garment. During the ceremony a Brahmin student, from the shore, asked solemnly, "What seest thou?" to which the answer was returned, "Sons and Cattle."[56] In all these cases there can be no doubt that it was the prolific nature of the Fish, a feature which it shares in common with the Dove, which inspired practice and intention.

Surely the effect of this cumulative body of evidence is to justify us in the belief that Fish and Fisher, being, as they undoubtedly are, Life symbols of immemorial antiquity, are, by virtue of their origin, entirely in their place in a sequence of in-

---

[52] Cf. Scheftelowitz, p. 338. Hagen, *Der Gral*, has argued that Wolfram's stone is such a meteoric stone, a Boetylus. I am not prepared to take up any position as to the exact nature of the stone itself, whether precious stone or meteor; the real point of importance being its Life-giving potency.

[53] *Op. cit.* p. 381.

[54] *Ibid.* p. 376 *et seq.*

[55] *Ibid.* p. 20.

[56] *Ibid.* p. 377.

cidents which there is solid ground for believing derive ultimately from a Cult of this nature. That Borron's Fish-meal, that the title of Fisher King, are not accidents of literary invention but genuine and integral parts of the common body of tradition which has furnished the incidents and *mise-en-scène* of the Grail drama. Can it be denied that, while from the standpoint of a Christian interpretation the character of the Fisher King is simply incomprehensible, from the standpoint of Folk-tale inadequately explained, from that of a Ritual survival it assumes a profound meaning and significance? He is not merely a deeply symbolic figure, but the essential centre of the whole cult, a being semi-divine, semi-human, standing between his people and land, and the unseen forces which control their destiny. If the Grail story be based upon a Life ritual the character of the Fisher King is of the very essence of the tale, and his title, so far from being meaningless, expresses, for those who are at pains to seek, the intention and object of the perplexing whole. The Fisher King is, as I suggested above, the very heart and centre of the whole mystery, and I contend that with an adequate interpretation of this enigmatic character the soundness of the theory providing such an interpretation may be held to be definitely proved.

CHAPTER X

The Secret of the Grail
(1) The Mysteries

STUDENTS of the Grail literature cannot fail to have
been impressed by a certain atmosphere of awe and
mystery which surrounds that enigmatic Vessel.
There is a secret connected with it, the revelation of
which will entail dire misfortune on the betrayer. If
spoken of at all it must be with scrupulous accuracy.
It is so secret a thing that no woman, be she wife or
maid, may venture to speak of it. A priest, or a man
of holy life might indeed tell the marvel of the Grail,
but none can hearken to the recital without shudder-
ing, trembling, and changing colour for very fear.

> *"The Grail's secret must be concealed*
> *And never by any man revealed,*
> *For as soon as this tale is told,*
> *It could happen to one so bold,*
> *If the teller should have a wife,*
> *Evil will follow him all his life.*
>
> . . . .
>
> *If Master Blihis does not lie*
> *This secret none should ever tell."[1]*

> *"But the marvel that he found here*
> *Which often made him shake with fear,*
> *He must never let anyone know,*

[1] *Elucidation*, ll. 4–9 and 12, 13.

> *He who tells it shall have great woe,*
> *For of the Grail it is the sign*
> *That he in pain and ills will pine*
> *Who reveals its secret to any man."*[2]

The above refers to Gawain's adventure at the Black Chapel, *en route* for the Grail castle.

The following is the answer given to Perceval by the maiden of the White Mule, after he has been overtaken by a storm in the forest. She tells him the mysterious light he beheld proceeded from the Grail, but on his enquiry as to what the Grail may be, refuses to give him any information.

> *"She said, 'Sire, it cannot be*
> *That I may tell this mystery,*
> *If a hundred times you ask*
> *I may not speak more of my task,*
> *For this would be too bold,*
> *It is too secret to be told.*
> *No lady, girl or maid may say it*
> *Nor may any man betray it*
> *Who is wedded to a wife.*
> *Only a man of holy life*
> *Or a priest of this may tell*
> *Revealing all its wondrous spell*
> *Which no one can ever hear*
> *Without turning pale with fear,*
> *Trembling, becoming a wretched sight,*
> *A man stricken by utter fright.'"*[3]

From this evidence there is no doubt that to the romance writers the Grail was something secret, mysterious and awful, the exact knowledge of which was reserved to a select few, and which was only to

[2] Potvin, ll. 19933–40. I quote from Potvin's edition as more accessible than the MSS., but the version of Mons is, on the whole, an inferior one.

[3] Potvin, ll. 28108–28.

be spoken of with bated breath, and a careful regard to strict accuracy.

But how does this agree with the evidence set forth in our preceding chapters? There we have been led rather to emphasize the close parallels existing between the characters and incidents of the Grail story, and a certain well-marked group of popular beliefs and observances, now very generally recognized as fragments of a once widespread Nature Cult. These beliefs and observances, while dating from remotest antiquity, have, in their modern survivals, of recent years, attracted the attention of scholars by their persistent and pervasive character, and their enduring vitality.

Yet, so far as we have hitherto dealt with them, these practices were, and are, popular in character, openly performed, and devoid of the special element of mystery which is so characteristic a feature of the Grail.

Nor, in these public Folk-ceremonies, these Spring festivals, Dances, and Plays, is there anything which, on the face of it, appears to bring them into touch with the central mystery of the Christian Faith. Yet the men who wrote these romances saw no incongruity in identifying the mysterious Food-providing Vessel of the *Bleheris-Gawain* version with the Chalice of the Eucharist, and in ascribing the power of bestowing Spiritual Life to that which certain modern scholars have identified as a *Wunsch-Ding*, a Folk-tale Vessel of Plenty.

If there be a mystery of the Grail surely the mystery lies here, in the possibility of identifying two objects which, apparently, lie at the very opposite poles of intellectual conception. What brought them together? Where shall we seek a connecting link? By what road did the romancers reach so strangely unexpected a goal?

It is, of course, very generally recognized that in the case of most of the pre-Christian religions, upon the nature and character of whose rites we possess reliable information, such rites possessed a two-fold character—*exoteric;* in celebrations openly and publicly performed, in which all adherents of that particular cult could join freely, the object of such public rites being to obtain some external and material benefit, whether for the individual worshipper, or for the community as a whole—*esoteric;* rites open only to a favoured few, the initiates, the object of which appears, as a rule, to have been individual rather than social, and *non*-material. In some cases, certainly, the object aimed at was the attainment of a conscious, ecstatic, union with the god, and the definite assurance of a future life. In other words there was the public worship, and there were the Mysteries.

Of late years there has been a growing tendency among scholars to seek in the Mysteries the clue which shall enable us to read aright the baffling riddle of the Grail, and there can be little doubt that, in so doing, we are on the right path. At the same time I am convinced that to seek that clue in those Mysteries which are at once the most famous, and the most familiar to the classical scholar, *i.e.*, the Eleusinian, is a fatal mistake. There are, as we shall see, certain essential, and radical, differences between the Greek and the Christian religious conceptions which, affecting as they do the root conceptions of the two groups, render it quite impossible that any form of the Eleusinian Mystery cult could have given such results as we find in the Grail legend.[4]

---

[4] This is to my mind the error vitiating much of Dr Nitze's later work, *e.g.*, the studies entitled *The Fisher-King in the Grail Romances* and *The Sister's Son, and the Conte del Graal.*

Cumont in his *Les Religions Orientales dans le Paganisme Romain,* speaking of the influence of the Mysteries upon Christianity, remarks acutely, "But when we speak of the mysteries, we should think of Hellenized Asia rather than of Greece proper, in spite of all the prestige that surrounds Eleusis. For the first Christian communities were established, shaped and developed in the midst of Oriental peoples—Semites, Phrygians, Egyptians."[5]

This is perfectly true, but it was not only the influence of *milieu,* not only the fact that the 'hellenized' faiths were, as Cumont points out, more advanced, richer in ideas and sentiments, more pregnant, more poignant, than the more strictly 'classic' faiths, but they possessed, in common with Christianity, certain distinctive features lacking in these latter.

If we were asked to define the special characteristic of the central Christian rite, should we not state it as being a Sacred meal of Communion in which the worshipper, not merely symbolically, but actually, partakes of, and becomes one with, his God, receiving thereby the assurance of eternal life? (*The Body of Our Lord Jesus Christ preserve thy body and soul unto everlasting life.*)

But it is precisely this conception which is lacking in the Greek Mysteries, and that inevitably, as Rohde points out: "The Eleusinian Mysteries in common with all Greek religion, differentiated clearly between gods and men, *"there is one race of men, another race of gods."* The attainment of union with the god, by way of ecstasy, as in other Mystery cults, is foreign to the Eleusinian idea. As Cumont puts it "The Greco-Roman deities rejoice in the perpetual calm and youth of Olympus, the Eastern deities die

[5] *Op. cit.* Introduction, p. x.

to live again."[6] In other words Greek religion lacks the Sacramental idea.

Thus even if we set aside the absence of a parallel between the ritual of the Greek Mysteries and the *mise-en-scène* of the Grail stories, Eleusis would be unable to offer us those essential elements which would have rendered possible a translation of the incidents of those stories into terms of high Christian symbolism. Yet we cannot refrain from the conclusion that there was something in the legend that not merely rendered possible, but actually invited, such a translation.

If we thus dismiss, as fruitless for our investigation, the most famous representative of the Hellenic Mysteries proper, how does the question stand with regard to those faiths to which Cumont is referring, the hellenized cults of Asia Minor?

Here the evidence, not merely of the existence of Mysteries, but of their widespread popularity, and permeating influence, is overwhelming; the difficulty is not so much to prove our case, as to select and coordinate the evidence germane to our enquiry.

Regarding the question as a whole it is undoubtedly true that, as Anrich remarks, "the extent of the literature devoted to the Mysteries stands in no relation whatever (*gar keinem Verhältniss*) to the importance in reality attached to them."[7] Later in the same connection, after quoting Clement of Alexandria's dictum "Mysteries such as divinity are entrusted to speech, not to writing," he adds; "*Setting such things down in writing is already almost profanation.*"[8] A just remark which it would be well if certain critics who make a virtue of refusing to ac-

---

[6] Rohde, *Psyche*, p. 293, and Cumont, *op. cit.* p. 44.

[7] Anrich, *Das alte Mysterien-Wesen in seinem Verhältniss zum Christentum*, p. 46.

[8] *Op. cit.* p. 136.

cept as evidence anything short of a direct and positive literary statement would bear in mind. There are certain lines of research in which, as Bishop Butler long since emphasized, probability must be our guide.

Fortunately, however, so far as our present research is concerned, we have more than probability to rely upon; not only did these Nature Cults with which we are dealing express themselves in Mystery terms, but as regards these special Mysteries we possess clear and definite information, and we know, moreover, that in the Western world they were, of all the Mystery faiths, the most widely spread, and the most influential.

As Sir J. G. Frazer has before now pointed out, there are parallel and over-lapping forms of this cult, the name of the god, and certain details of the ritual, may differ in different countries, but whether he hails from Babylon, Phrygia, or Phoenicia, whether he be called Tammuz, Attis, or Adonis, the main lines of the story are fixed, and invariable. Always he is young and beautiful, always the beloved of a great goddess; always he is the victim of a tragic and untimely death, a death which entails bitter loss and misfortune upon a mourning world, and which, for the salvation of that world, is followed by a resurrection. Death and Resurrection, mourning and rejoicing, present themselves in sharp antithesis in each and all of the forms.

We know the god best as Adonis, for it was under that name that, though not originally Greek, he became known to the Greek world, was adopted by them with ardour, carried by them to Alexandria, where his feast assumed the character of a State solemnity; under that name his story has been enshrined in Art, and as Adonis he is loved and lamented to this day. The Adonis ritual may be held to be the classic form of the cult.

But in Rome, the centre of Western civilization, it was otherwise: there it was the Phrygian god who was in possession; the dominating position held by the cult of Attis and the *Magna Mater*, and the profound influence exercised by that cult over better known, but subsequently introduced, forms of worship, have not, so far, been sufficiently realized.

The first of the Oriental cults to gain a footing in the Imperial city, the worship of the *Magna Mater* of Pessinonte was, for a time, rigidly confined within the limits of her sanctuary. The orgiastic ritual of the priests of Kybele made at first little appeal to the more disciplined temperament of the Roman population. By degrees, however, it won its way, and by the reign of Claudius had become so popular that that emperor instituted public feasts in honour of Kybele and Attis, feasts which were celebrated at the Spring solstice, March 15th–27th.[9]

As the public feast increased in popularity, so did the Mystery feast, of which the initiated alone were privileged to partake, acquire a symbolic significance: the foods partaken of became "a food of spiritual life, intended to sustain the initiate in the trials of existence." Philosophers boldy utilized the framework of the Attis cult as the vehicle for imparting their own doctrines, "When Neoplatonism triumphs, the Phrygian fable will become the traditional mould into which subtle exegetes will boldly pour their philosophical speculations on the creative and fruitful principles of all material forms, and on the deliverance of the divine spirit which is submerged in the corruption of this terrestrial world."[10]

Certain of the Gnostic sects, both pre- and post-

[9] Cumont, *op. cit.* p. 84.
[10] *Op. cit.* pp. 104, 105.

Christian, appear to have been enthusiastic participants in the Attis mysteries;[11] Hepding, in his *Attis* study, goes so far as to refer to Bishop Aberkios, to whose enigmatic epitaph our attention was directed in the last chapter, as *"the priest of Attis."*[12]

Another element aided in the diffusion of the ritual. Of all the Oriental cults which journeyed Westward under the aegis of Rome none was so deeply rooted or so widely spread as the originally Persian cult of Mithra—the popular religion of the Roman legionary. But between the cults of Mithra and of Attis there was a close and intimate alliance. In parts of Asia Minor the Persian god had early taken over features of the Phrygian deity. "As soon as we can establish the presence of the Persian cult in Italy, we find it intimately united with that of the Great Mother of Pessinonte."[13] The union between Mithra and the goddess Anâhita was held to be the equivalent of that subsisting between the two great Phrygian deities Attis-Kybele. The most ancient Mithreum known, that at Ostia, was attached to the Metroon, the temple of Kybele. At Saalburg the ruins of the two temples are but a few steps apart. "There is every reason to believe that the cult of the Iranian god and that of the Phrygian goddess existed in close communion throughout the whole extent of the empire."[14]

A proof of the close union of the two cults is afforded by the mystic rite of the Taurobolium, which was practised by both, and which, in the West, at least, seems to have passed from the temples of the Mithra to those of the *Magna Mater*. At the same time Cumont remarks that the actual rite

[11] Cf. Anrich, *op. cit.* p. 81.
[12] Hepding, *Attis*, p. 189.
[13] Cumont, *Mystères de Mithra*, pp. 19 and 78.
[14] *Ibid.* p. 188.

seems to have been practised in Asia from a great antiquity, before Mithraism had attributed to it a spiritual significance. It is thus possible that the rite had earlier formed a part of the Attis initiation, and had been temporarily disused.[15]

We shall see that the union of the Mithra-Attis cults becomes of distinct importance when we examine, (*a*) the spiritual significance of these rituals, and their elements of affinity with Christianity, (*b*) their possible diffusion in the British Isles.

But now what do we know of the actual details of the Attis mysteries? The first and most important point was a Mystic Meal, at which the food partaken of was served in the sacred vessels, the tympanum, and the cymbals. The formula of an Attis initiate was *"I have eaten from the tympanum, I have drunk from the cymbals."* As I have remarked above, the food thus partaken of was a Food of Life—*"The devotees of Attis believed, in fact, that they were eating a magic food of life from the sacred vessels of their cult."*[16]

Dieterich in his interesting study entitled *Eine Mithrasliturgie* refers to this meal as the centre of the whole religious action.

Further, in some mysterious manner, the fate of the initiate was connected with, and dependent upon, the death and resurrection of the god. The Christian writer Firmicius Maternus, at one time himself an initiate, has left an account of the ceremony, without, however, specifying whether the deity in question was Attis or Adonis—as Dieterich remarks "What he relates can be applied both to the devotees of Attis and to those of Adonis."

This is what he says: *"On a certain night the image is placed, lying on its back, on a litter, and the dev-*

15 *Ibid.* pp. 190 *et seq.*
16 *Vide* Hepding, *Attis*, Chap. 4, for details.

*otees mourn it with rhymic lamentations. At length,
when they have satisfied themselves with this pretended lamentation, a light is brought in. Then the
throats of all those who were weeping are anointed
by the priest, and after they have been anointed, he
slowly murmurs these words to them:*

*'Have courage, O initiates of the saviour-god,
For there will be salvation for us from our toils—'"*

on which Dieterich remarks: "The salvation of the
initiates depends on the deliverance of the god."[17]

Hepding holds that in some cases there was an
actual burial, and awakening with the god to a new
life.[18] In any case it is clear that the successful issue
of the test of initiation was dependent upon the
resurrection and revival of the god.

Now is it not clear that we have here a close parallel with the Grail romances? In each case we have
a common, and mystic, meal, in which the food partaken of stands in close connection with the holy
vessels. In the Attis feast the initiates actually ate
and drank from these vessels; in the romances the
Grail community never actually eat from the Grail
itself, but the food is, in some mysterious and unexplained manner, supplied by it. In both cases it
is a *Lebens-Speise,* a Food of Life. This point is especially insisted upon in the *Parzival,* where the
Grail community never become any older than they
were on the day they first beheld the Talisman.[19] In
the Attis initiation the proof that the candidate has
successfully passed the test is afforded by the revival

---

[17] Dieterich, *Eine Mithrasliturgie,* p. 174.

[18] Hepding, *op. cit.* p. 196.

[19] Cf. my *Legend of Sir Perceval,* Vol. II. p. 313. Hepding
mentions (*op. cit.* p. 174) among the *sacra* of the goddess
Phrygium ferrum, which he suggests was the knife with which
the Archigallus wounded himself on the 'Blood' day. Thus it
is possible that the primitive ritual may have contained a knife.

of the god—in the Grail romances the proof lies in the healing of the Fisher King.

Thus, while deferring for a moment any insistence on the obvious points of parallelism with the Sacrament of the Eucharist, and the possibilities of Spiritual teaching inherent in the ceremonies, necessary links in our chain of argument, we are, I think, entitled to hold that, even when we pass beyond the outward *mise-en-scène* of the story—the march of incident, the character of the King, his title, his disability, and relation to his land and folk—to the inner and deeper significance of the tale, the Nature Cults still remain reliable guides; it is their inner, their esoteric, ritual which will enable us to bridge the gulf between what appears at first sight the wholly irreconcilable elements of Folk-tale and high Spiritual mystery.

CHAPTER XI

The Secret of the Grail
(2) The Naassene Document

WE have now seen that the Ritual which, as we have postulated, lies, in a fragmentary and distorted condition, at the root of our existing Grail romances, possessed elements capable of assimilation with a religious system which the great bulk of its modern adherents would unhesitatingly declare to be its very antithesis. That Christianity might have borrowed from previously existing cults certain outward signs and symbols, might have accommodated itself to already existing Fasts and Feasts, may be, perforce has had to be, more or less grudgingly admitted; that such a *rapprochement* should have gone further, that it should even have been inherent in the very nature of the Faith, that, to some of the deepest thinkers of old, Christianity should have been held for no new thing but a fulfilment of the promise enshrined in the Mysteries from the beginning of the world, will to many be a strange and startling thought. Yet so it was, and I firmly believe that it is only in the recognition of this one-time claim of essential kinship between Christianity and the Pagan Mysteries that we shall find the key to the Secret of the Grail.

And here at the outset I would ask those readers who are inclined to turn with feelings of contemptuous impatience from what they deem an unprofit-

able discussion of idle speculations which have little
or nothing to do with a problem they hold to be one
of purely literary interest, to be solved by literary
comparison and criticism, and by no other method,
to withhold their verdict till they have carefully
examined the evidence I am about to bring forward,
evidence which has never so far been examined in
this connection, but which if I am not greatly mistaken provides us with clear and unmistakable proof
of the actual existence of a ritual in all points analogous to that indicated by the Grail romances.

In the previous chapter we have seen that there
is evidence, and abundant evidence, not merely of
the existence of Mysteries connected with the worship of Adonis-Attis, but of the high importance
assigned to such Mysteries; at the time of the birth
of Christianity they were undoubtedly the most
popular and the most influential of the foreign cults
adopted by Imperial Rome. In support of this statement I quoted certain passages from Cumont's *Religions Orientales*, in which he touches on the subject:
here are two other quotations which may well serve
as introduction to the evidence we are about to examine. "Researches on the doctrines and practices
common to Christianity and the Oriental Mysteries
almost invariably go back, beyond the limits of the
Roman Empire, to the Hellenized East. It is there we
must seek the key of enigmas still unsolved—The
essential fact to remember is that the Eastern religions had diffused, first anterior to, then parallel
with, Christianity, doctrines which acquired with
this latter a universal authority in the decline of the
ancient world. The preaching of Asiatic priests prepared in their own despite the triumph of the
Church."[1]

But the triumph of the new Faith once assured

[1] Cumont, *op. cit.* Introd. pp. xx and xxi.

the organizing, dominating, influence of Imperial Rome speedily came into play. Christianity, originally an Eastern, became a Western, religion, the 'Mystery' elements were frowned upon, kinship with pre-Christian faiths ignored, or denied; where the resemblances between the cults proved too striking for either of these methods such resemblances were boldly attributed to the invention of the Father of Lies himself, a cunning snare whereby to deceive unwary souls. Christianity was carefully trimmed, shaped, and forced into an Orthodox mould, and anything that refused to adapt itself to this drastic process became by that very refusal anathema to the righteous.

Small wonder that, under such conditions, the early ages of the Church were marked by a fruitful crop of Heresies, and heresy-hunting became an intellectual pastime in high favour among the strictly orthodox. Among the writers of this period whose works have been preserved Hippolytus, Bishop of Portus in the early years of the third century, was one of the most industrious. He compiled a voluminous treatise, entitled *Philosophumena,* or *The Refutation of all Heresies,* of which only one MS. and that of the fourteenth century, has descended to us. The work was already partially known by quotations, the first Book had been attributed to Origen, and published in the *editio princeps* of his works. The text originally consisted of ten Books, but of these the first three, and part of the fourth, are missing from the MS. The Origen text supplies part of the lacuna, but two entire Books, and part of a third are missing.

Now these special Books, we learn from the Introduction, dealt with the doctrines and Mysteries of the Egyptians and Chaldaeans, whose most sacred secrets Hippolytus boasts that he has divulged.

Curiously enough, not only are these Books lacking but in the Epitome at the beginning of Book x. the summary of their contents is also missing, a significant detail, which, as has been suggested by critics, looks like a deliberate attempt on the part of some copyist to suppress the information contained in the Books in question. Incidentally this would seem to suggest that the worthy bishop was not making an empty boast when he claimed to be a revealer of secrets.

But what is of special interest to us is the treatment meted out to the Christian Mystics, whom Hippolytus stigmatizes as heretics, and whose teaching he deliberately asserts to be simply that of the Pagan Mysteries. He had come into possession of a secret document belonging to one of these sects, whom he calls the Naassenes; this document he gives in full, and it certainly throws a most extraordinary light upon the relation which this early Christian sect held to exist between the New, and the Old, Faith. Mr G. R. S. Mead, in his translation of the Hermetic writings entitled *Thrice-Greatest Hermes*, has given a careful translation and detailed analysis of this most important text, and it is from his work that I shall quote.

So far as the structure of the document is concerned Mr Mead distinguishes three stages.

(*a*) An original Pagan source, possibly dating from the last half of the first century B.C., but containing material of earlier date.

(*b*) The working over of this source by a Jewish Mystic whom the critic holds to have been a contemporary of Philo.

(*c*) A subsequent working over, with additions, by a Christian Gnostic (Naassene), in the middle of the second century A.D. Finally the text was edited by Hippolytus, in the *Refutation*, about 222

A.D. Thus the ground covered is roughly from 50 B.C. to 220 A.D.[2]

In the translation given by Mr Mead these successive layers are distinguished by initial letters and difference of type, but these distinctions are not of importance for us; what we desire to know is what was really held and taught by these mystics of the Early Church. Mr Mead, in his introductory remarks, summarizes the evidence as follows: "The claim of these Gnostics was practically that Christianity, or rather the Good News of The Christ, was precisely the consummation of the inner doctrine of the Mystery-institutions of all the nations: the end of them all was the revelation of the Mystery of Man."[3] In other words the teaching of these Naassenes was practically a synthesis of all the Mystery-religions, and although Hippolytus regards them as nothing more than devotees of the cult of the *Magna Mater*, we shall see that, while their doctrine and teaching were undoubtedly based mainly upon the doctrine and practices of the Phrygian Mysteries, they practically identified the deity therein worshipped, *i.e.*, Attis, with the presiding deity of all the other Mysteries.

Mr Mead draws attention to the fact that Hippolytus places these Naassenes in the fore-front of his *Refutation;* they are the first group of Heretics with whom he deals, and we may therefore conclude that he considered them, if not the most important, at least the oldest, of such sectaries.[4]

With these prefatory remarks it will be well to let the document speak for itself. It is of considerable length, and, as we have seen, of intricate construction. I shall therefore quote only those sections

[2] *Thrice-Greatest Hermes,* Vol. I. p. 195.
[3] *Op. cit.* p. 141.
[4] *Op. cit.* p. 142.

which bear directly upon the subject of our investigation; any reader desirous of fuller information
can refer to Mr Mead's work, or to the original text
published by Reitzenstein.[5]

At the outset it will be well to understand that
the central doctrine of all these Mysteries is what
Reitzenstein sums up as "the doctrine of the Man,
the Heavenly Man, the Son of God, who descends
and becomes a slave of the Fate Sphere: the Man
who, though originally endowed with all power,
descends into weakness and bondage, and has to
win his own freedom, and regain his original state.
This doctrine is not Egyptian, but seems to have
been in its origin part and parcel of the Chaldean
Mystery-tradition and was widely spread in Hellenistic circles."[6]

Thus, in the introductory remarks prefixed by
Hippolytus to the document he is quoting he asserts
that the Naassenes honour as the Logos of all
universals Man, and Son of Man—"and they divide
him into three, for they say he has a mental, psychic,
and choïc aspect; and they think that the Gnosis
of this Man is the beginning of the possibility of
knowing God, saying, 'The beginning of Perfection
is the Gnosis of Man, but the Gnosis of God is
perfected Perfection.' All these, mental, psychic,
and earthy, descended together into one Man, Jesus,
the Son of Mary."[7]

Thus the *Myth of Man,* the Mystery of Generation,
is the subject matter of the document in question,
and this myth is set forth with reference to all the
Mysteries, beginning with the Assyrian.

[5] *Op. cit.* pp. 146 *et seq.* Reitzenstein, *Die Hellenistischen
Mysterien Religionen,* Leipzig, 1910, gives the document in
the original. There is also a translation of Hippolytus in the
Ante-Nicene Library.
[6] Quoted by Mead, *op. cit.* p. 138.
[7] *Op. cit.* pp. 146, 147.

Paragraph 5 runs: "Now the Assyrians call this Mystery Adonis, and whenever it is called Adonis it is Aphrodite who is in love with and desires Soul so-called, and Aphrodite is Genesis according to them."[8]

But in the next section the writer jumps from the Assyrian to the Phrygian Mysteries, saying, "But if the Mother of the Gods emasculates Attis, she too regarding him as the object of her love, it is the Blessed Nature above of the super-Cosmic, and Aeonian spaces which calls back the masculine power of Soul to herself."[9]

In a note to this Mr Mead quotes from *The Life of Isidorus*: "I fell asleep and in a vision Attis seemed to appear to me, and on behalf of the Mother of gods to initiate me into the feast called Hilario, a mystery which discloses the way of our salvation from Hades." Throughout the document reference is continually made to the Phrygians and their doctrine of Man. The Eleusinian Mysteries are then treated of as subsequent to the Phrygian, "after the Phrygians, the Athenians," but the teaching is represented as being essentially identical.

We have then a passage of great interest for our investigation, in which the Mysteries are sharply divided into two classes, and their separate content clearly defined. There are—"the little Mysteries, those of the Fleshly Generation, and after men have been initiated into them they should cease for a while and become initiated in the Great, Heavenly, Mysteries—for this is the Gate of Heaven, and this is the House of God, where the Good God dwells alone, into which House no impure man shall

---

[8] *Op. cit.* p. 151.
[9] *Op. cit.* p. 152. Mr Mead concludes that there is here a lacuna in the original.

come."[10] Hippolytus remarks that "these Naassenes say that the performers in theatres, they too, neither say nor do anything without design—for example, when the people assemble in the theatre, and a man comes on the stage clad in a robe different from all others, with lute in hand on which he plays, and thus chants the Great Mysteries, not knowing what he says:

'Whether blest Child of Kronos, or of Zeus, or of
    Great Rhea,
Hail Attis, thou mournful song of Rhea!
Assyrians call thee thrice-longed-for Adonis;
All Egypt calls thee Osiris;
The Wisdom of Hellas names thee Men's Heavenly
    Horn;
The Samothracians call thee august Adama;
The Haemonians, Korybas;
The Phrygians name thee Papa sometimes;
At times again Dead, or God, or Unfruitful, or
    Aipolos;
Or Green Reaped Wheat-ear;
Or the Fruitful that Amygdalas brought forth,
Man, Piper—Attis!'

This is the Attis of many forms, of whom they sing as follows:

'Of Attis will I sing, of Rhea's Beloved,
Not with the booming of bells,
Nor with the deep-toned pipe of Idaean Kuretes;
But I will blend my song with Phoebus' music of
    the lyre;
Evoi, Evan,—for thou art Pan, thou Bacchus art, and
    Shepherd of bright stars!' "[11]

[10] *Op. cit.* p. 181. In a note Mr Mead says of the Greater Mysteries, "presumably the candidate went through some symbolic rite of death and resurrection."

[11] *Op. cit.* pp. 185, 186. I would draw especial attention to

On this Hippolytus comments: "For these and suchlike reasons these Naassenes frequent what are called the Mysteries of the Great Mother, believing that they obtain the clearest view of the universal Mystery from the things done in them."

And after all this evidence of elaborate syncretism, this practical identification of all the Mystery-gods with the Vegetation deity Adonis-Attis, we are confronted in the concluding paragraph, after stating that "the True Gate is Jesus the Blessed," with this astounding claim, from the pen of the latest redactor, "And of all men we alone are Christians, accomplishing the Mystery at the Third Gate."[12]

Now what conclusions are to be drawn from this document which, in its entirety, Mr Mead regards as "the most important source we have for the higher side (regeneration) of the Hellenistic Mysteries"?

First of all, does it not provide a complete and overwhelming justification of those scholars who have insisted upon the importance of these Vegetation cults—a justification of which, from the very nature of their studies, they could not have been aware?

Sir James Frazer, and those who followed him, have dealt with the public side of the cult, with its importance as a recognized vehicle for obtaining material advantages; it was the social, rather than the individual, aspect which appealed to them. Now we find that in the immediate *pre-* and *post-*Christian

this passage in view of the present controversy as to the Origin of Drama. It looks as if the original writer of the document (and this section is in the Pagan Source) would have inclined to the views of Sir Gilbert Murray, Miss Harrison, and Mr Cornford rather than to those championed by their sarcastic critic, Sir W. Ridgeway.

[12] *Op. cit.* p. 190.

era these cults were considered not only most potent factors for assuring the material prosperity of land and folk, but were also held to be the most appropriate vehicle for imparting the highest religious teaching. The Vegetation deities, Adonis-Attis, and more especially the Phrygian god, were the chosen guides to the knowledge of, and union with, the supreme Spiritual Source of Life, of which they were the communicating medium.

We must remember that though the document before us is, in its actual form, the expression of faith of a discredited 'Christian-Gnostic' sect, the essential groundwork upon which it is elaborated belongs to a period anterior to Christianity, and that the Ode in honour of Attis quoted above not only forms part of the original source, but is, in the opinion of competent critics, earlier than the source itself.

I would also recall to the memory of the reader the passage previously quoted from Cumont, in which he refers to the use made by the Neo-Platonist philosophers of the Attis legend, as the mould into which they poured their special theories of the universe, and of generation.[13] Can the importance of a cult capable of such far-reaching developments be easily exaggerated? Secondly, and of more immediate importance for our investigation, is it not evident that we have here all the elements necessary for a mystical development of the Grail tradition? The Exoteric side of the cult gives us the Human, the Folk-lore, elements—the Suffering King; the Waste Land; the effect upon the Folk; the task that lies before the hero; the group of Grail symbols. The Esoteric side provides us with the Mystic Meal, the Food of Life, connected in some mysterious way with a Vessel which is the centre of the cult; the

[13] *Vide supra*, p. 144.

combination of that vessel with a Weapon, a combination bearing a well-known 'generative' significance; a double initiation into the source of the lower and higher spheres of Life; the ultimate proof of the successful issue of the final test in the restoration of the King. I would ask any honest-minded critic whether any of the numerous theories previously advanced has shown itself capable of furnishing so comprehensive a solution of the *ensemble* problem?

At the same time it should be pointed out that the acceptance of this theory of the origin of the story in no way excludes the possibility of the introduction of other elements during the period of romantic evolution. As I have previously insisted,[14] not all of those who handled the theme knew the real character of the material with which they were dealing, while even among those who did know there were some who allowed themselves considerable latitude in their methods of composition; who did not scruple to introduce elements foreign to the original *Stoff*, but which would make an appeal to the public of the day. Thus while Bleheris who, I believe, really held a tradition of the original cult, contented himself with a practically simple recital of the initiations, later redactors, under the influence of the Crusades, and the Longinus legend —possibly also actuated by a desire to substitute a more edifying explanation than that originally offered—added a directly Christian interpretation of the Lance. As it is concerning the Lance alone that Gawain asks, the first modification must have been at this point; the bringing into line of the twin symbol, the Vase, would come later.

The fellowship, it may even be, the rivalry, between the two great Benedictine houses of Fes-

[14] Cf. *Legend of Sir Perceval*, Vol. II. Chapters 10 and 11.

camp and Glastonbury, led to the redaction, in the interests of the latter, of a *Saint-Sang* legend, parallel to that which was the genuine possession of the French house.[15] For we must emphasize the fact that the original Joseph-Glastonbury story is a *Saint-Sang*, and not a *Grail* legend. A phial containing the Blood of Our Lord was said to have been buried in the tomb of Joseph—surely a curious fate for so precious a relic—and the Abbey never laid claim to the possession of the Vessel of the Last Supper.[16] Had it done so it would certainly have become a noted centre of pilgrimage—as Dr Brugger acutely remarks such relics are "visited, not sought after."

But there is reason to believe that the kindred Abbey of Fescamp had developed its genuine *Saint-Sang* legend into a Grail romance, and there is critical evidence to lead us to suppose that the text we know as *Perlesvaus* was, in its original form, now it is to be feared practically impossible to reconstruct, connected with that Abbey. As we have it, this alone, of all the Grail romances, connects the hero alike with Nicodemus, and with Joseph of Arimathea, the respective protagonists of the *Saint-Sang* legends; while its assertion that the original Latin text was found in a holy house situated in marshes, the burial place of Arthur and Guenevere, unmistakably points to Glastonbury.

In any case, when Robert de Borron proposed to himself the task of composing a trilogy on the subject the Joseph legend was already in a developed form, and a fresh element, the combination of the Grail legend with the story of a highly popular Folk-tale hero, known in this connection as Perceval (though he has had many names), was established.

---

[15] Cf. my *Quest of the Holy Grail*, Bell, 1913, Chap. 4, for summary of evidence on this point.

[16] Cf. Heinzel, *Alt-Franz. Gral-Romanen*, p. 72.

Borron was certainly aware of the real character of his material; he knew the Grail cult as Christianized Mystery, and, while following the romance development, handled the theme on distinctively religious lines, preserving the Mystery element in its three-fold development, and equating the Vessel of the Mystic Feast with the Christian Eucharist. From what we now know of the material it seems certain that the equation was already established, and that Borron was simply stating in terms of romance what was already known to him in terms of Mystery. In face of the evidence above set forth there can no longer be any doubt that the Mystic Feast of the Nature cults really had, and that at a very early date, been brought into touch with the Sacrament of the Eucharist.

But to Chrétien de Troyes the story was romance, pure and simple. There was still a certain element of awe connected with Grail, and Grail Feast, but of the real meaning and origin of the incidents he had, I am convinced, no idea whatever. Probably many modifications were already in his source, but the result so far as his poem is concerned is that he duplicated the character of the Fisher King; he separated both, Father and Son, from the Wasted Land, transferring the responsibility for the woes of Land and Folk to the Quester, who, although his failure might be responsible for their continuance, never had anything to do with their origin. He bestowed the wound of the Grail King, deeply significant in its original conception and connection, upon Perceval's father, a shadowy character, entirely apart from the Grail tradition. There is no trace of the Initiation elements in his poem, no Perilous Chapel, no welding of the Sword. We have here passed completely and entirely into the land of romance, the doors of the Temple are closed behind

us. It is the story of Perceval li Gallois, not the Ritual
of the Grail, which fills the stage, and with the story
of Perceval there comes upon the scene a crowd of
Folk-tale themes, absolutely foreign to the Grail
itself.

Thus we have not only the central theme of the
lad reared in woodland solitude, making his entrance
into a world of whose ordinary relations he is
absolutely and ludicrously ignorant, and the traditional illustrations of the results of that ignorance,
such as the story of the Lady of the Tent and the
stolen ring; but we have also the sinister figure of
the Red Knight with his Witch Mother; the three
drops of blood upon the snow, and the ensuing
love trance; pure Folk-tale themes, mingled with the
more chivalric elements of the rescue of a distressed
maiden, and the vanquishing in single combat of
doughty antagonists, Giant, or Saracen. One and all
of them elements offering widespread popular parallels, and inviting the unwary critic into paths
which lead him far astray from the goal of his quest,
the Grail castle. I dispute in no way the possible
presence of Celtic elements in this complex. The
Lance may well have borrowed at one time features
from early Irish tradition, at another details obviously closely related to the Longinus legend. It
is even possible that, as Burdach insists, features
of the Byzantine Liturgy may have coloured the
representation of the Grail procession, although,
for my own part, I consider such a theory highly
improbable in view of the facts that (*a*) Chrétien's
poem otherwise shows no traces of Oriental influence; (*b*) the 'Spear' in the Eastern rite is simply
a small spear-shaped knife; (*c*) the presence of the
lights is accounted for by the author of *Sone de
Nansai* on the ground of a Nativity legend, the
authenticity of which was pointed out by the late

M. Gaston Paris; (*d*) it is only in the later prose form that we find any suggestion of a Grail Chapel, whereas were the source of the story really to be found in the Mass, such a feature would certainly have had its place in the earliest versions. But in each and all these cases the solution proposed has no relation to other features of the story; it is consequently of value *in*, and *per se*, only, and cannot be regarded as valid evidence for the source of the legend as a whole. In the process of transmutation from Ritual to Romance, the kernel, the Grail legend proper, may be said to have formed for itself a shell composed of accretions of widely differing *provenance*. It is the legitimate task of criticism to analyse such accretions, and to resolve them into their original elements, but they are accretions, and should be treated as such, not confounded with the original and essential material. After upwards of thirty years spent in careful study of the Grail legend and romances I am firmly and entirely convinced that the root origin of the whole bewildering complex is to be found in the Vegetation Ritual, treated from the esoteric point of view as a Life-Cult, *and in that alone.* Christian Legend, and traditional Folk-tale, have undoubtedly contributed to the perfected romantic *corpus*, but they are in truth subsidiary and secondary features; a criticism that would treat them as original and primary can but defeat its own object; magnified out of proportion they become stumbling-blocks upon the path, instead of sign-posts towards the goal.

CHAPTER XII

Mithra and Attis

THE fact that there was, at a very early date, among a certain sect of Christian Gnostics, a well-developed body of doctrine, based upon the essential harmony existing between the Old Faith and the New, which claimed by means of a two-fold Initiation to impart to the inner circle of its adherents the secret of life, physical and spiritual, being, in face of the evidence given in the previous chapter, placed beyond any possible doubt, we must now ask, is there any evidence that such teaching survived for any length of time, or could have penetrated to the British Isles, where, in view of the priority of the *Bleheris-Gawain* form, the Grail legend, as we know it, seems to have originated? I think there is at least presumptive evidence of such preservation, and transmission. I have already alluded to the close connection existing between the Attis cult, and the worship of the popular Persian deity, Mithra, and have given quotations from Cumont illustrating this connection; it will be worth while to study the question somewhat more closely, and discover, if possible, the reason for this intimate alliance.

On the face of it there seems to be absolutely no reason for the connection of these cults; the two deities in no way resemble each other; the stories connected with them have no possible analogy; the root conception is widely divergent.

With the character of the deity we know as

Adonis, or Attis, we are now thoroughly familiar. In the first instance it seems to be the human element in the myth which is most insisted upon. He is a mortal youth beloved by a great goddess; only after his tragic death does he appear to assume divine attributes, and, alike in death and resurrection, become the accepted personification of natural energies.

Baudissin, *Adonis und Esmun,* remarks that Adonis belongs to "a class of beings of a very indefinite kind, which clearly stand above men but below the great gods, and which possess less individuality than these."[1] Such a criticism applies of course equally to Attis.

Mithra, on the other hand, occupies an entirely different position. Cumont, in his *Mystères de Mithra,* thus describes him; he is "the spirit of celestial light. He is not the sun or the moon or the stars, but with the help of these thousand orbs and these two thousand eyes, he watches over the world."[2]

His beneficent activities might seem to afford a meeting ground with the Vegetation gods—"He grants increase and abundance, he enlarges the flocks, he gives fertility and life."[3]

This summary may aptly be compared with the lament for Tammuz, quoted in Chapter 3.

But the worship of Mithra in the form in which it spread throughout the Roman Empire, Mithra as the god of the Imperial armies, the deity beloved of the Roman legionary, was in no sense of this concrete and material type.

This is how Cumont sums up the main features. Mithra is the Mediator, who stands between "the

[1] *Op. cit.* p. 71.
[2] *Op. cit.* p. 3.
[3] *Op. cit.* p. 4.

inaccessible and unknowable God, who reigns in the ethereal spheres, and the human race which suffers here below."—"He is the Logos emanating from God and participating in all His power, who, after having formed the world as a demiurge, continues to watch over it." The initiates must practice a strict chastity. "Resistance to sensuality was one of the aspects of the struggle against the principle of evil—fundamentally, Mithraic dualism served a very pure and efficacious morality."[4]

Finally, Mithraism taught the resurrection of the body—Mithra will descend upon earth, and will revive all men. All will issue from their graves, resume their former appearance and recognize each other. All will be united in one great assembly, and the good will be separated from the evil. Then in one supreme sacrifice Mithra will immolate the divine bull, and mixing its fat with the consecrated wine will offer to the righteous the cup of Eternal Life.[5]

The final parallel with the Messianic Feast described in Chapter 9 is too striking to be overlooked.

The celestial nature of the deity is also well brought out in the curious text edited by Dieterich from the great Magic Papyrus of the Bibliothèque Nationale, and referred to in a previous chapter. This text purports to be a formula of initiation, and we find the aspirant ascending through the Seven Heavenly Spheres, to be finally met by Mithra who brings him to the presence of God. So in the Mithraic temples we find seven ladders, the ascent of which by the Initiate typified his passage to the seventh and supreme Heaven.[6]

---

[4] Cumont, *op. cit.* pp. 129–141 *et seq.*
[5] *Op. cit.* p. 148.
[6] Dieterich, *Eine Mithrasliturgie,* the text is given with

Bousset points out that the original idea was that of three Heavens above which was Paradise; the conception of Seven Heavens, ruled by the seven Planets, which we find in Mithraism, is due to the influence of Babylonian sidereal cults.[7]

There is thus a marked difference between the two initiations; the Attis initiate dies, is possibly buried, and revives with his god; the Mithra initiate rises direct to the celestial sphere, where he is met and welcomed by his god. There is here no evidence of the death and resurrection of the deity.

What then is the point of contact between the cults that brought them into such close and intimate relationship?

I think it must be sought in the higher teaching, which, under widely differing external mediums, included elements common to both. In both cults the final aim was the attainment of spiritual and eternal life. Moreover, both possessed essential features which admitted, if they did not encourage, an assimilation with Christianity. Both of them, if forced to yield ground to their powerful rival, could, with a fair show of reason, claim that they had been not vanquished, but fulfilled, that their teaching had, in Christianity, attained its normal term.

The extracts given above will show the striking analogy between the higher doctrine of Mithraism, and the fundamental teaching of its great rival, a resemblance that was fully admitted, and which became the subject of heated polemic. Greek philosophers did not hesitate to establish a parallel entirely favourable to Mithraism, while Christian apologists insisted that such resemblances were the

translation and is followed by an elaborate commentary. The whole study is most interesting and suggestive.

[7] Cf. Bousset, *Der Himmelfahrt der Seele, Archiv für Religionswissenschaft*, Vol. IV.

work of the Devil, a line of argument which, as we have seen above, they had already adopted with regard to the older Mysteries. It is a matter of historical fact that at one moment the religious fate of the West hung in the balance, and it was an open question whether Mithraism or Christianity would be the dominant Creed.[8]

On the other hand we have also seen that certainly one early Christian sect, the Naassenes, while equally regarding the Logos as the centre of their belief, held the equivalent deity to be Attis, and frequented the Phrygian Mysteries as the most direct source of spiritual enlightenment, while the teaching as to the Death and Resurrection of the god, and the celebration of a Mystic Feast, in which the worshippers partook of the Food and Drink of Eternal Life, offered parallels to Christian doctrine and practice to the full as striking as any to be found in the Persian faith.

I would therefore submit that it was rather through the medium of their inner, Esoteric, teaching, that the two faiths, so different in their external practice, preserved so close and intimate a connection and that, by the medium of that same Esoteric teaching, both alike came into contact with Christianity, and, in the case of the Phrygian cult, could, and actually did, claim identity with it.

Baudissin in his work above referred to suggests that the Adonis cult owed its popularity to its higher, rather than to its lower, elements, to its suggestion of ever-renewing life, rather than to the satisfaction of physical desire to be found in it.[9] Later evidence seems to prove that he judged correctly.

We may also note that the Attis Mysteries were

[8] Cumont, *op. cit.* pp. 199 *et seq.*
[9] *Adonis und Esmun,* p. 521.

utilized by the priests of Mithra for the initiation of women who were originally excluded from the cult of the Persian god. Cumont remarks that this, an absolute rule in the Western communities, seems to have had exceptions in the Eastern.[10] Is it possible that the passage quoted in the previous chapter, in which Perceval is informed that no woman may speak of the Grail, is due to contamination with the Mithra worship? It does not appear to be in harmony with the prominent position assigned to women in the Grail ritual, the introduction of a female Grail messenger, or the fact that (with the exception of Merlin in the Borron text) it is invariably a maiden who directs the hero on his road to the Grail castle, or reproaches him for his failure there.

But there is little doubt that, separately, or in conjunction, both cults travelled to the furthest borders of the Roman Empire. The medium of transmission is very fully discussed by Cumont in both of the works referred to. The channel appears to have been three-fold. First, commercial, through the medium of Syrian merchants. As ardently religious as practically business-like, the Syrians introduced their native deities wherever they penetrated, "founding their chapels at the same time as their counting-houses."[11]

Secondly, there was social penetration—by means of the Asiatic slaves, who formed a part of most Roman households, and the State *employés,* such as officers of customs, army paymasters, etc., largely recruited from Oriental sources.

Thirdly, and most important, were the soldiers, the foreign legions, who, drawn mostly from the

[10] Cf. Mead, *op. cit.* p. 179, note; Cumont, *Mystères de Mithra,* p. 183.
[11] Cumont, *Les Religions Orientales,* pp. 160 *et seq.*

Eastern parts of the Empire, brought their native deities with them. Cumont signalizes as the most active agents of the dispersion of the cult of Mithra, Soldiers, Slaves, and Merchants.[12]

As far North as Hadrian's Dyke there has been found an inscription in verse in honour of the goddess of Hierapolis, the author a prefect, probably, Cumont remarks, the officer of a cohort of Hamii, stationed in this distant spot. Dedications to Melkart and Astarte have been found at Corbridge near Newcastle. The Mithraic remains are practically confined to garrison centres, London, York, Chester, Caerleon-on-Usk, and along Hadrian's Dyke.[13] From the highly interesting map attached to the Study, giving the sites of ascertained Mithraic remains, there seems to have been such a centre in Pembrokeshire.

Now in view of all this evidence is it not at least possible that the higher form of the Attis cult, that in which it was known and practised by early Gnostic Christians, may have been known in Great Britain? Scholars have been struck by the curiously unorthodox tone of the Grail romances, their apparent insistence on a succession quite other than the accredited Apostolic tradition, and yet, according to the writers, directly received from Christ Himself. The late M. Paulin Paris believed that the source of this peculiar feature was to be found in the struggle for independence of the early British Church; but, after all, the differences of that Church with Rome affected only minor points of discipline: the date of Easter, the fashion of tonsure of the clergy, nothing which touched vital doctrines of the Faith. Certainly the British Church never

[12] *Mystères de Mithra,* p. 77.
[13] *Les Religions Orientales,* pp. 166, 167; *Mystères de Mithra,* p. 57.

claimed the possession of a revelation *à part*. But
if the theory based upon the evidence of the
Naassene document be accepted such a presentation
can well be accounted for. According to Hippolytus the doctrines of the sect were derived from
James, the brother of Our Lord, and Clement of
Alexandria asserts that "The Lord imparted the
Gnosis to James the Just, to John and to Peter,
after His Resurrection; these delivered it to the
rest of the Apostles, and they to the Seventy."[14]
Thus the theory proposed in these pages will account
not only for the undeniable parallels existing between the Vegetation cults and the Grail romances,
but also for the Heterodox colouring of the latter,
two elements which at first sight would appear
to be wholly unconnected, and quite incapable
of relation to a common source.

Nor in view of the persistent vitality and survival,
even to our own day, of the Exoteric practices can
there be anything improbable in the hypothesis
of a late survival of the Esoteric side of the ritual.
Cumont points out that the worship of Mithra was
practised in the fifth century in certain remote
cantons of the Alps and the Vosges—*i.e.*, at the
date historically assigned to King Arthur. Thus it
would not be in any way surprising if a tradition
of the survival of these semi-Christian rites at this
period also existed.[15] In my opinion it is the tradition of such a survival which lies at the root, and
explains the confused imagery, of the text we know
as the *Elucidation*. I have already, in my short study
of the subject, set forth my views; as I have since
found further reasons for maintaining the correct-

[14] Mead, *op. cit.* pp. 147, 148 and note.
[15] Without entering into indiscreet details I may say that
students of the Mysteries are well aware of the continued
survival of this ritual under circumstances which correspond
exactly with the indications of two of our Grail romances.

ness of the solution proposed, I will repeat it here.[16]

The text in question is found in three of our existing Grail versions: in the MS. of Mons; in the printed edition of 1530; and in the German translation of Wisse-Colin. It is now prefixed to the poem of Chrétien de Troyes, but obviously, from the content, had originally nothing to do with that version.

It opens with the passage quoted above (p. 137) in which Master Blihis utters his solemn warning against revealing the secret of the Grail. It goes on to tell how aforetime there were maidens dwelling in the hills[17] who brought forth to the passing traveller food and drink. But King Amangons outraged one of these maidens, and took away from her her golden Cup:

> *"One of the maidens he took by force*
> *And from her seized her golden cup."*[18]

His knights, when they saw their lord act thus, followed his evil example, forced the fairest of the maidens, and robbed them of their cups of gold. As a result the springs dried up, the land became waste, and the court of the Rich Fisher, which had filled the land with plenty, could no longer be found.

For 1000 years the land lies waste, till, in the days of King Arthur, his knights find maidens wandering in the woods, each with her attendant knight. They joust, and one, Blihos-Bliheris, vanquished by Gawain, comes to court and tells how these maidens

---

16 *The Quest of the Holy Grail,* pp. 110 *et seq.*

17 Professor A. C. L. Brown, *Notes on Celtic Cauldrons of Plenty,* n. p. 249, translates this 'wells,' an error into which the late Mr Alfred Nutt had already fallen. Wisse-Colin translates correctly, *berg, gebirge.*

18 I suspect that the robbery of the Golden Cup was originally a symbolic expression for the outrage offered.

are the descendants of those ravished by King Amangons and his men, and how, could the court of the Fisher King, and the Grail, once more be found, the land would again become fertile. Blihos-Bliheris is, we are told, so entrancing a story-teller that none at court could ever weary of listening to his words.

The natural result, which here does not immediately concern us, was that Arthur's knights undertook the quest, and Gawain achieved it. Now at first sight this account appears to be nothing but a fantastic fairy-tale (as such Professor Brown obviously regarded it), and although the late Dr Sebastian Evans attempted in all seriousness to find a historical basis for the story in the events which provoked the pronouncement of the Papal Interdict upon the realm of King John, and the consequent deprivation of the Sacraments, I am not aware that anyone took the solution seriously. Yet, on the basis of the theory now set forth, is it not possible that there may be a real foundation of historical fact at the root of this wildly picturesque tale? May it not be simply a poetical version of the disappearance from the land of Britain of the open performance of an ancient Nature ritual? A ritual that lingered on in the hills and mountains of Wales as the Mithra worship did in the Alps and Vosges, celebrated as that cult habitually was, in natural caverns, and mountain hollows? That it records the outrage offered by some, probably local, chieftain to a priestess of the cult, an evil example followed by his men, and the subsequent cessation of the public celebration of the rites, a cessation which in the folk-belief would certainly be held sufficient to account for any subsequent drought that might affect the land? But the ritual, in its higher, esoteric, form was still secretly observed, and the tradition, alike of its disappearance as a public cult, and of its persistence in some carefully hidden strong-hold, was handed on in the families of those who had been, perhaps still were, officiants of these rites.

That among the handers on of the torch would be the descendants of the outraged maidens, is most probable.

The sense of mystery, of a real danger to be faced, of an overwhelming Spiritual gain to be won, were of the essential nature of the tale. It was the very mystery of Life which lay beneath the picturesque wrappings; small wonder that the Quest of the Grail became the synonym for the highest achievement that could be set before men, and that when the romantic evolution of the Arthurian tradition reached its term, this supreme adventure was swept within the magic circle. The knowledge of the Grail was the utmost man could achieve, Arthur's knights were the very flower of manhood, it was fitting that to them the supreme test be offered. That the man who first told the story, and boldly, as befitted a born teller of tales, wedded it to the Arthurian legend, was himself connected by descent with the ancient Faith, himself actually held the Secret of the Grail, and told, in purposely romantic form, that of which he knew, I am firmly convinced, nor do I think that the time is far distant when the missing links will be in our hand, and we shall be able to weld once more the golden chain which connects Ancient Ritual with Medieval Romance.

CHAPTER XIII

The Perilous Chapel

STUDENTS of the Grail romances will remember that in many of the versions the hero—sometimes it is a heroine—meets with a strange and terrifying adventure in a mysterious Chapel, an adventure which, we are given to understand, is fraught with extreme peril to life. The details vary: sometimes there is a Dead Body laid on the altar; sometimes a Black Hand extinguishes the tapers; there are strange and threatening voices, and the general impression is that this is an adventure in which supernatural, and evil, forces are engaged.

Such an adventure befalls Gawain on his way to the Grail castle.[1] He is overtaken by a terrible storm, and coming to a Chapel, standing at a crossways in the middle of a forest, enters for shelter. The altar is bare, with no cloth, or covering, nothing is thereon but a great golden candlestick with a tall taper burning within it. Behind the altar is a window, and as Gawain looks a Hand, black and hideous, comes through the window, and extinguishes the taper, while a voice makes lamentation loud and dire, beneath which the very building rocks. Gawain's horse shies for terror, and the knight, making the sign of the Cross, rides out of the Chapel, to find the storm abated, and the great wind fallen. Thereafter the night was calm and clear.

[1] MS. B.N. 12576, ff. 87vo et seq. A translation will be found in my *Sir Gawain at the Grail Castle*, pp. 13–15.

In the *Perceval* section of Wauchier and Manessier we find the same adventure in a dislocated form.[2]

Perceval, seeking the Grail castle, rides all day through a heavy storm, which passes off at nightfall, leaving the weather calm and clear. He rides by moonlight through the forest, till he sees before him a great oak, on the branches of which are lighted candles, ten, fifteen, twenty, or twenty-five. The knight rides quickly towards it, but as he comes near the lights vanish, and he only sees before him a fair little Chapel, with a candle shining through the open door. He enters, and finds on the altar the body of a dead knight, covered with a rich samite, a candle burning at his feet.

Perceval remains some time, but nothing happens. At midnight he departs; scarcely has he left the Chapel when, to his great surprise, the light is extinguished.

The next day he reaches the castle of the Fisher King, who asks him where he passed the preceding night. Perceval tells him of the Chapel; the King sighs deeply, but makes no comment.

Wauchier's section breaks off abruptly in the middle of this episode; when Manessier takes up the story he gives explanations of the Grail, etc., at great length, explanations which do not at all agree with the indications of his predecessor. When Perceval asks of the Chapel he is told it was built by Queen Brangemore of Cornwall, who was later murdered by her son Espinogres, and buried beneath the altar. Many knights have since been slain there, none know by whom, save it be by the Black Hand which appeared and put out the light. (As we saw above it had not appeared.) The enchantment can only be put an end to if a valiant knight will fight

[2] MS. B.N. 12576, ff. 150*vo*, 222, 238*vo*.

the Black Hand, and, taking a veil kept in the Chapel, will dip it in holy water, and sprinkle the walls, after which the enchantment will cease.

At a much later point Manessier tells how Perceval, riding through the forest, is overtaken by a terrible storm. He takes refuge in a Chapel which he recognizes as that of the Black Hand. The Hand appears, Perceval fights against and wounds it; then appears a Head; finally the Devil in full form who seizes Perceval as he is about to seek the veil of which he has been told. Perceval makes the sign of the Cross, on which the Devil vanishes, and the knight falls insensible before the altar. On reviving he takes the veil, dips it in holy water, and sprinkles the walls within and without. He sleeps there that night, and the next morning, on waking, sees a belfry. He rings the bell, upon which an old man, followed by two others, appears. He tells Perceval he is a priest, and has buried 3000 knights slain by the Black Hand; every day a knight has been slain, and every day a marble tomb stands ready with the name of the victim upon it. Queen Brangemore founded the cemetery, and was the first to be buried within it. (But according to the version given earlier she was buried beneath the altar.) We have here evidently a combination of two themes, Perilous Chapel and Perilous Cemetery, originally independent of each other. In other MSS. the Wauchier adventure agrees much more closely with the Manessier sequel, the Hand appearing, and extinguishing the light. Sometimes the Hand holds a bridle, a feature probably due to contamination with a Celtic Folk-tale, in which a mysterious Hand (here that of a giant) steals on their birth-night a Child, and a foal.[3]

[3] Cf. here Prof. Kittredge's monograph *Arthur and Gorlagon.*

These *Perceval* versions are manifestly confused and dislocated, and are probably drawn from more than one source.

In the *Queste* Gawain and Hector de Maris come to an old and ruined Chapel where they pass the night. Each has a marvellous dream. The next morning, as they are telling each other their respective visions, they see, "a Hand, showing unto the elbow, and was covered with red samite, and upon that hung a bridle, not rich, and held within the fist a great candle that burnt right clear, and so passed afore them, and entered into the Chapel, and then vanished away, and they wist not where."[4] This seems to be an unintelligent borrowing from the *Perceval* version.

We have, also, a group of visits to the Perilous Chapel, or Perilous Cemetery, which appear to be closely connected with each other. In each case the object of the visit is to obtain a portion of the cloth which covers the altar, or a dead body lying upon the altar. The romances in question are the *Perlesvaus,* the prose *Lancelot,* and the *Chevalier à deux Espées.*[5] The respective protagonists being Perceval's sister, Sir Lancelot, and the young Queen of Garadigan, whose city has been taken by King Ris and who dares the venture to win her freedom.

In the first case the peril appears to lie in the Cemetery, which is surrounded by the ghosts of knights slain in the forest, and buried in unconsecrated ground. The *Lancelot* version is similar, but here the title is definitely *Perilous Chapel.* In the last version there is no hint of a Cemetery.

In the *Lancelot* version there is a dead knight on the altar, whose sword Lancelot takes in addition

[4] Cf. Malory, Book xvi. Chap. 2.
[5] Cf. *Perlesvaus,* Branch xv. sections xii.–xx.; Malory, Book vi. Chap. 15; *Chevalier à deux Espées,* ll. 531 *et seq.*

to the piece of cloth. In the poem a knight is brought in, and buried before the altar; the young queen, after cutting off a piece of the altar cloth, uncovers the body, and buckles on the sword. There is no mention of a Hand in any of the three versions, which appear to be late and emasculated forms of the theme.

The earliest mention of a Perilous Cemetery, as distinct from a Chapel, appears to be in the Chastel Orguellous section of the *Perceval*, a section probably derived from a very early stratum of Arthurian romantic tradition. Here Arthur and his knights, on their way to the siege of Chastel Orguellous, come to the *Vergier des Sepoltures,* where they eat with the Hermits, of whom there are a hundred and more.

> *"There is none could ever tell*
> *Of the graveyard's marvellous spell,*
> *Its wonders so diverse and great*
> *No one alive could now relate*
> *Or even dream that there could be*
> *Such things as these for men to see."*[6]

But there is no hint of a Perilous Chapel here.

The adventures of Gawain in the *Atre Perilleus,*[7] and of Gawain and Hector in the *Lancelot* of the final cyclic prose version, are of the most *banal* description; the theme, originally vivid and picturesque, has become watered down into a meaningless adventure of the most conventional type.

But originally a high importance seems to have been attached to it. If we turn back to the first version given, that of which Gawain is the hero, we shall find that special stress is laid on this

[6] B.N. 12576, fo. 74*vo*.
[7] Cf. B.N. MS. 1433, ff. 10, 11, and the analysis and remarks in my *Legend of Sir Lancelot,* p. 219 and note.

adventure, as being part of 'the Secret of the Grail,' of which no man may speak without grave danger.[8] We are told that, but for Gawain's loyalty and courtesy, he would not have survived the perils of that night. In the same way Percival, before reaching the Fisher King's castle, meets a maiden, of whom he asks the meaning of the lighted tree, Chapel, etc. She tells him it is all part of the *saint secret* of the Grail.[9] Now what does this mean? Unless I am much mistaken the key is to be found in a very curious story related in the *Perlesvaus*, which is twice referred to in texts of a professedly historical character. The tale runs thus. King Arthur has fallen into slothful and *fainéant* ways, much to the grief of Guenevere, who sees her lord's fame and prestige waning day by day. In this crisis she urges him to visit the Chapel of Saint Austin, a perilous adventure, but one that may well restore his reputation. Arthur agrees; he will take with him only one squire; the place is too dangerous. He calls a youth named Chaus, the son of Yvain the Bastard, and bids him be ready to ride with him at dawn. The lad, fearful of over-sleeping, does not undress, but lies down as he is in the hall. He falls asleep—and it seems to him that the King has wakened and gone without him. He rises in haste, mounts and rides after Arthur, following, as he thinks, the track of his steed. Thus he comes to a forest glade, where he sees a Chapel, set in the midst of a grave-yard. He enters, but the King is not there; there is no living thing, only the body of a knight on a bier, with tapers burning in golden candlesticks at head and foot. Chaus takes out one of the tapers, and thrusting the golden candlestick betwixt hose and thigh, remounts and rides back in search of the King. Before he has gone far he meets

8 Cf. passage in question quoted on p. 137.
9 B.N. 12576, fo. 150vo.

a man, black, and foul-favoured, armed with a
large two-edged knife. He asks, has he met King
Arthur? The man answers, No, but he has met
him, Chaus; he is a thief and a traitor; he has stolen
the golden candlestick; unless he gives it up he shall
pay for it dearly. Chaus refuses, and the man smites
him in the side with the knife. With a loud cry the
lad awakes, he is lying in the hall at Cardoil,
wounded to death, the knife in his side and the
golden candlestick still in his hose.

He lives long enough to tell the story, confess,
and be shriven, and then dies. Arthur, with the
consent of his father, gives the candlestick to the
church of Saint Paul, then newly founded, "for he
would that this marvellous adventure should every-
where be known, and that prayer should be made
for the soul of the squire."[10]

The pious wish of the King seems to have been
fulfilled, as the story was certainly well known, and
appears to have been accepted as a genuine tradition. Thus the author of the *Histoire de Fulk Fitz-
Warin* gives a *résumé* of the adventure, and asserts
that the Chapel of Saint Austin referred to was situated in Fulk's patrimony, *i.e.*, in the tract known as
the Blaunche Launde, situated in Shropshire, on the
border of North Wales. As source for the tale he
refers to *Le Graal, le lyvre de le Seint Vassal,* and
goes on to state that here King Arthur recovered *sa
bounté et sa valur* when he had lost his knighthood
and fame. This obviously refers to the *Perlesvaus* romance, though whether in its present, or in an earlier
form, it is impossible to say. In any case the author
of the *Histoire* evidently thought that the Chapel in
question really existed, and was to be located in

[10] *Perlesvaus*, Branch I. sections III., IV.

Shropshire.[11] But John of Glastonbury also refers to the story, and he connects it with Glastonbury.[12]

Now how can we account for so wild, and at first sight so improbable, a tale assuming what we may term a semi-historical character, and becoming connected with a definite and precise locality?—a feature which is, as a rule, absent from the Grail stories.

At the risk of startling my readers I must express my opinion that it was because the incidents recorded were a reminiscence of something which had actually happened, and which, owing to the youth, and possible social position, of the victim, had made a profound impression upon the popular imagination.

For this is the story of an initiation (or perhaps it would be more correct to say the test of fitness for an initiation) *carried out on the astral plane, and reacting with fatal results upon the physical.*

We have already seen in the Naassene document that the Mystery ritual comprised a double initiation, the Lower, into the mysteries of generation, *i.e.*, of physical Life; the higher, into the Spiritual Divine Life, where man is made one with God.[13]

Some years ago I offered the suggestion that the test for the primary initiation, that into the sources of physical life, would probably consist in a contact with the horrors of physical death, and that the tradition of the Perilous Chapel, which survives in the Grail romances in confused and contaminated form, was a reminiscence of the test for this lower initiation.[14] This would fully account for the importance

[11] Cf. my notes on the subject, *Romania*, Vol. XLIII. pp. 420–426.
[12] Cf. Nitze, *Glastonbury and the Holy Grail*, where the reference is given.
[13] *Vide supra*, p. 155.
[14] Cf. *Legend of Sir Perceval*, Vol. II. p. 261. I suggested then that the actual initiation would probably consist in en-

ascribed to it in the *Bleheris-Gawain* form, and for the asserted connection with the Grail. It was not till I came to study the version of the *Perlesvaus*, with a view to determining its original *provenance*, that I recognized its extreme importance for critical purposes. The more one studies this wonderful legend the more one discovers significance in what seem at first to be entirely independent and unrelated details. If the reader will refer to my Notes on the *Perlesvaus*, above referred to, he will find that the result of an investigation into the evidence for *locale* pointed to the conclusion that the author of the *Histoire de Fulk Fitz-Warin* and most probably also the author of the *Perlesvaus* before him, were mistaken in their identification, that there was no tradition of any such Chapel in Shropshire, and consequently no tale of its foundation, such as the author of the *Histoire* relates. But I was also able to show that further north, in Northumberland, there was also a Blanchland, connected with the memory of King Arthur, numerous dedications to Saint Austin, and a tradition of that Saint driving out the local demons closely analogous to the tale told of the presumed Shropshire site. I therefore suggested that inasmuch as the *Perlesvaus* represented Arthur as holding his court at Cardoil (Carlisle), the Northern Blanchland, which possessed a Chapel of Saint Austin, and lay within easy reach, was probably the original site rather than the Shropshire Blaunche Launde, which had no Chapel, and was much further away.

---

lightenment into the meaning of Lance and Cup, in their sexual juxtaposition. I would now go a step further, and suggest that the identification of the Lance with the weapon of Longinus may quite well have replaced the original explanation as given by Bleheris. In *The Quest,* Oct. 1916, I have given, under the title 'The Ruined Temple,' a hypothetical reconstruction of the Grail Initiation.

Now in view of the evidence set forth in the last chapter, is it not clear that this was a locality in which these semi-Pagan, semi-Christian, rites, might, *prima facie,* be expected to linger on? It is up here, along the Northern border, that the Roman legionaries were stationed; it is here that we find monuments and memorials of their heathen cults; obviously this was a locality where the demon-hunting activities of the Saint might find full scope for action. I would submit that there is at least presumptive evidence that we may here be dealing with the survival of a genuine tradition.

And should any of my readers find it difficult to believe that, even did initiations take place, and even were they of a character that involved a stern test of mental and physical endurance—and I imagine most scholars would admit that there was, possibly, more in the original institutions, than, let us say, in a modern admission to Free-Masonry—yet it is 'a far cry' from pre-Christian initiations to Medieval Romance, and a connection between the two is a rash postulate, I would draw their attention to the fact that, quite apart from our Grail texts, we possess a romance which is, plainly, and blatantly, nothing more or less than such a record. I refer, of course, to *Owain Miles,* or *The Purgatory of Saint Patrick,* where we have an account of the hero, after purification by fasting and prayer, descending into the Nether World, passing through the abodes of the Lost, finally reaching Paradise, and returning to earth after Three Days, a reformed and regenerated character.[15]

---

[15] *Owain Miles,* edited from the unique MS. by Turnbull and Laing, Edinburgh, 1837. *The Purgatory of Saint Patrick* will be found in Horstmann's Southern Legendary. I have given a modern English rendering of part of *Owain Miles* in my *Chief Middle-English Poets,* published by Houghton Mifflin Co., Boston, U.S.A.

"Then with his monks the Prior anon,
With Crosses and with Gonfanon
Went to that hole forthright,
Thro' which Knight Owain went below,
There, as of burning fire the glow,
They saw a gleam of light;
And right amidst that beam of light
He came up, Owain, God's own knight,
By this knew every man
That he in Paradise had been,
And Purgatory's pains had seen,
And was a holy man."

Now if we turn to Bousset's article *Himmelfahrt der Seele,* to which I have previously referred (p. 167), we shall find abundant evidence that such a journey to the Worlds beyond was held to be a high spiritual adventure of actual possibility—a venture to be undertaken by those who, greatly daring, felt that the attainment of actual knowledge of the Future Life was worth all the risks, and they were great and terrible, which such an enterprise involved.

Bousset comments fully on Saint Paul's claim to have been 'caught up into the Third Heaven' and points out that such an experience was the property of the Rabbinical school to which Saul of Tarsus had belonged, and was brought over by him from his Jewish past; such experiences were rare in Orthodox Christianity.[16] According to Jewish classical tradition but one Rabbi had successfully passed the test, other aspirants either failing at a preliminary stage, or, if they persevered, losing their senses permanently. The practice of this ecstatic ascent ceased among Jews in the second century A.D.

Bousset also gives instances of the soul leaving the body for three days, and wandering through other

16 Cf. *op. cit.* pp. 148 *et seq.*

worlds, both good and evil, and also discusses the origin of the bridge which must be crossed to reach Paradise, both features characteristic of the *Owain* poem.[17] In fact the whole study is of immense importance for a critical analysis of the sources of the romance in question.

And here I would venture to beg the adherents of the 'Celtic' school to use a little more judgment in their attribution of sources. Visits to the Otherworld are not *always* derivations from Celtic Fairy-lore. Unless I am mistaken the root of this theme is far more deeply imbedded than in the shifting sands of Folk and Fairy tale. I believe it to be essentially a Mystery tradition; the Otherworld is not a myth, but a reality, and in all ages there have been souls who have been willing to brave the great adventure, and to risk all for the chance of bringing back with them some assurance of the future life. Naturally these ventures passed into tradition with the men who risked them. The early races of men became semi-mythic, their beliefs, their experiences, receded into a land of mist, where their figures assumed fantastic outlines, and the record of their deeds departed more and more widely from historic accuracy.

The poets and dreamers wove their magic webs, and a world apart from the world of actual experience came to life. But it was not all myth, nor all fantasy; there was a basis of truth and reality at the foundation of the mystic growth, and a true criticism will not rest content with wandering in these enchanted lands, and holding all it meets with for the outcome of human imagination.

The truth may lie very deep down, but it is there, and it is worth seeking, and Celtic fairy-tales, charming as they are, can never afford a satisfactory, or

[17] *Op. cit.* pp. 155 and 254.

abiding, resting place. I, for one, utterly refuse to accept such as an adequate goal for a life's research. A path that leads but into a Celtic Twilight can only be a by-path, and not the King's Highway!

The Grail romances repose eventually, not upon a poet's imagination, but upon the ruins of an august and ancient ritual, a ritual which once claimed to be the accredited guardian of the deepest secrets of Life. Driven from its high estate by the relentless force of religious evolution—for after all Adonis, Attis, and their congeners, were but the 'half-gods' who must needs yield place when 'the Gods' themselves arrive—it yet lingered on; openly, in Folk practice, in Fast and Feast, whereby the well-being of the land might be assured; secretly, in cave or mountain-fastness, or island isolation, where those who craved for a more sensible (not necessarily sensuous) contact with the unseen Spiritual forces of Life than the orthodox development of Christianity afforded, might, and did, find satisfaction.

Were the Templars such? Had they, when in the East, come into touch with a survival of the Naassene, or some kindred sect? It seems exceedingly probable. If it were so we could understand at once the puzzling connection of the Order with the Knights of the Grail, and the doom which fell upon them. That they were held to be Heretics is very generally admitted, but in what their Heresy consisted no one really knows; little credence can be attached to the stories of idol worship often repeated. If their Heresy, however, were such as indicated above, a Creed which struck at the very root and vitals of Christianity, we can understand at once the reason for punishment, and the necessity for secrecy. In the same way we can now understand why the Church knows nothing of the Grail; why that Vessel, surrounded as it is with an atmosphere of reverence and awe, equated with the central Sacrament of the Christian Faith, yet appears in no Legendary, is figured in no picture, comes on the scene in no Passion Play. The Church of the eleventh and twelfth centuries knew well what the Grail was, and we, when we realize its genesis and true lineage, need no longer wonder why a theme, for some short space so famous and so fruitful a source of literary inspiration, vanished utterly and completely from the world of literature.

Were Grail romances forbidden? Or were they merely discouraged? Probably we shall never know, but of this one thing we may be sure, the Grail is a living force, it will never die; it may indeed sink out of sight, and, for centuries even, disappear from the field of literature, but it will rise to the surface again, and become once more a theme of vital inspiration even as, after slumbering from the days of Malory, it woke to new life in the nineteenth century, making its fresh appeal through the genius of Tennyson and Wagner.

CHAPTER XIV

The Author

HAVING now completed our survey of the various elements which have entered into the composite fabric of the Grail Legend, the question naturally arises where, and when, did that legend assume romantic form, and to whom should we ascribe its literary origin?

On these crucial points the evidence at our disposal is far from complete, and we can do little more than offer suggestions towards the solution of the problem.

With regard to the first point, that of locality, the evidence is unmistakably in favour of a Celtic, specifically a Welsh, source. As a literary theme the Grail is closely connected with the Arthurian tradition. The protagonist is one of Arthur's knights, and the hero of the earlier version, Gawain, is more closely connected with Arthur than are his successors, Perceval and Galahad. The Celtic origin of both Gawain and Perceval is beyond doubt; and the latter is not merely a Celt, but is definitely Welsh; he is always 'li Gallois.' Galahad I hold to be a literary, and not a traditional, hero; he is the product of deliberate literary invention, and has no existence outside the frame of the later cyclic redactions. It is not possible at the present moment to say whether the *Queste* was composed in the British Isles, or on the continent, but we may safely lay it down as a basic principle that the original Grail heroes are of insular origin, and that the Grail legend, in its romantic, and literary, form is closely connected with British pseudo-historical tradition.

The beliefs and practices of which, if the theory maintained in these pages be correct, the Grail stories offer a more or less coherent survival can be shown, on the evidence of historic monuments, and surviving Folk-customs, to have been popular throughout the area of the British Isles; while, with regard to the higher teaching of which I hold these practices to have been the vehicle, Pliny comments upon the similarity existing between the ancient Magian Gnosis and the Druidical Gnosis of Gaul and Britain, an indication which, in the dearth of accurate information concerning the teaching of the Druids, is of considerable value.[1]

As we noted in the previous chapter, an interesting parallel exists between Wales, and localities, such as the Alps, and the Vosges, where we have definite proof that these Mystery cults lingered on after they had disappeared from public celebration. The Chart appended to Cumont's *Monuments de Mithra* shows Mithraic remains in precisely the locality where we have reason to believe certain of the *Gawain* and *Perceval* stories to have originated.

As to the date of origin, that, of course, is closely connected with the problem of authorship; if we can, with any possibility, identify the author we can approximately fix the date. So far as the literary evidence is concerned, we have no trace of the story before the twelfth century, but when we do meet with it, it is already in complete, and crystallized, form. More, there is already evidence of competing versions; we have no existing Grail romance which

---

[1] Cf. Mead, *Thrice Greatest Hermes,* Vol. III. p. 295. On this point the still untranslated *corpus* of Bardic poetry may possibly throw light.

we can claim to be free from contamination, and representing in all respects the original form.

There is no need here to go over old, and well-trodden, ground; in my studies of the *Perceval* Legend, and in the later popular *résumé* of the evidence,[2] *The Quest of the Holy Grail*, I have analysed the texts, and shown that, while the poem of Chrétien de Troyes is our earliest surviving literary version, there is the strongest possible evidence that Chrétien, as he himself admits, was not inventing, but re-telling, an already popular tale.[3] The Grail Quest was a theme which had been treated not once nor twice, but of which numerous, and conflicting, versions were already current, and, when Wauchier de Denain undertook to complete Chrétien's unfinished work, he drew largely upon these already existing forms, regardless of the fact that they not only contradicted the version they were ostensibly completing, but were impossible to harmonize with each other.

It is of importance for our investigation, however, to note that where Wauchier does refer to a definite source, it is to an evidently important and already famous collection of tales, *Le Grant Conte,* comprising several 'Branches,' the hero of the collection being not Chrétien's hero, Perceval, but Gawain, who, both in pseudo-historic and romantic tradition, is far more closely connected with the Arthurian legend, occupying, as he does, the traditional position of nephew, Sister's Son, to the monarch who is the centre of the cycle; even as Cuchullinn is sister's son to Conchobar, Diarmid to Finn, Tristan to Mark, and Roland to Charlemagne. In fact this relationship was

[2] *The Quest of the Holy Grail* (*Quest* series, Bell, 1913).
[3] On the point that Chrétien was treating an already popular theme, cf. Brugger, *Enserrement Merlin,* I. (*Zeitschrift für Franz. Sprache,* XXIX.).

so obviously required by tradition that we find Perceval figuring now as sister's son to Arthur, now to the Grail King, according as the Arthurian, or the Grail, tradition dominates the story.[4]

The actual existence of such a group of tales as those referred to by Wauchier derives confirmation from our surviving *Gawain* poems, as well as from the references in the *Elucidation,* and on the evidence at our disposal I have ventured to suggest the hypothesis of a group of poems, dealing with the adventures of Gawain, his son, and brother, the *ensemble* being originally known as *The Geste of Syr Gawayne,* a title which, in the inappropriate form *The Jest of Sir Gawain,* is preserved in the English version of that hero's adventure with the sister of Brandelis.[5] So keen a critic as Dr Brugger has not hesitated to accept the theory of the existence of this *Geste,* and is of opinion that the German poem *Diû Crône* may, in part at least, be derived from this source.

The central adventure ascribed to Gawain in this group of tales is precisely the visit to the Grail castle to which we have already referred, and we have pointed out that the manner in which it is related, its directness, simplicity, and conformity with what we know of the Mystery teaching presumably involved, taken in connection with the personality of the hero, and his position in Arthurian romantic tradition, appear to warrant us in assigning to it the position of priority among the conflicting versions we possess.

At two points in the re-telling of these *Gawain* tales Wauchier definitely refers to the author by name, Bleheris. On the second occasion he states

[4] That is, the relationship is due to romantic tradition, not to Mystery survival, as Dr Nitze maintains.
[5] Cf. *Romania,* Vol. xxxiii. pp. 333 *et seq.*

categorically that this Bleheris was of Welsh birth
and origin, *né et engenuïs en Galles,* and that he
told the tale in connection with which the statement
is made to a certain Comte de Poitiers, whose favourite story it was, he loved it above all others, which
would imply that it was not the only tale Bleheris
had told him.[6]

As we have seen in a previous chapter, the *Elucidation* prefaces its account of the Grail Quest by a
solemn statement of the gravity of the subject to be
treated, and a warning of the penalties which would
follow on a careless revelation of the secret. These
warnings are put into the mouth of a certain Master
Blihis, concerning whom we hear no more. A little
further on in the poem we meet with a knight,
Blihos-Bliheris, who, made prisoner by Gawain, re-
veals to Arthur and his court the identity of the
maidens wandering in the woods, of the Fisher King,
and the Grail, and is so good a story-teller that none
can weary of listening to his tales.[7]

Again, in the fragmentary remains of Thomas's
Tristan we have a passage in which the poet refers,
as source, to a certain Bréri, who knew "all the feats,
and all the tales, of all the kings, and all the counts
who had lived in Britain."[8]

Finally, Giraldus Cambrensis refers to "that famous story-teller," Bledhericus, who had lived
"shortly before our time" and whose renown he evidently takes for granted was familiar to his readers.

Now are we to hold that the Bleheris who, according to Wauchier, had told tales concerning Gawain, and Arthur's court, one of which tales was
certainly the Grail adventure; the Master Blihis, who

---

[6] Cf. *Legend of Sir Perceval,* Vol. I. Chap. 12, for the
passages referred to, also article in *Romania,* XXXIII.

[7] Cf. my *Quest of the Holy Grail,* pp. 110 *et seq.*

[8] Cf. *Tristan* (Bédier's ed.), Vol. I. l. 2120.

knew the Grail mystery, and gave solemn warning against its revelation; the Blihos-Bliheris, who knew the Grail, and many other tales; the Bréri, who knew all the legendary tales concerning the princes of Britain; and the famous story-teller Bledhericus, of whom Giraldus speaks, are distinct and separate personages, or mere inventions of the separate writers, or do all these passages refer to one and the same individual, who, in that case, may well have deserved the title *famosus ille fabulator?*

With regard to the attitude taken up by certain critics, that no evidential value can be attached to these references, I would point out that when Medieval writers quote an authority for their statements they, as a rule, refer to a writer whose name carries weight, and will impress their readers; they are offering a guarantee for the authenticity of their statements. The special attribution may be purely fictitious but the individual referred to enjoys an established reputation. Thus, the later cyclic redactions of the Arthurian romances are largely attributed to Walter Map, who, in view of his public position, and political activities, could certainly never have had the leisure to compose one half of the literature with which he is credited! In the same way Robert de Borron, Chrétien de Troyes, Wolfram von Eschenbach, are all referred to as sources without any justification in fact. Nor is it probable that Wauchier, who wrote on the continent, and who, if he be really Wauchier de Denain, was under the patronage of the Count of Flanders, would have gone out of his way to invent a Welsh source.

Judging from analogy, the actual existence of a personage named Bleheris, who enjoyed a remarkable reputation as a story-teller, is, *prima facie,* extremely probable.[9]

[9] A critic of my *Quest* volume remarks that "we have as

But are these references independent, was there
more than one Bleheris? I think not. The name is a
proper, and not a family, name. In the latter case it
might be possible to argue that we were dealing
with separate members of a family, or group, of
bardic poets, whose office it was to preserve, and re-

---

little faith in Wauchier's appeal to a Welshman Bleheris as
source for his continuation of Chrétien's *'Perceval'* as we
have in Layamon's similar appeal to Bede and St Austin at
the beginning of the *'Brut.'* " The remark seems to me singularly inept, there is no parallel between the cases. In the first
place Layamon does not refer to Bede and St Austin as
source, but as *models,* a very different thing. Then the statement is discredited by the fact that we possess the writings
of these men, and know them to be of another character than
Metrical Chronicles. In the case of Wauchier his reference
does not stand alone; it is one of a group, and that group
marked by an extraordinary unanimity of statement; whoever Bleheris may have been he was certainly possessed of
two definite qualifications—he knew a vast number of tales,
and he possessed a remarkable gift of narration, *i.e.,* he was
a story-teller, *par excellence.* Thus he was, *a priori,* a probable
source for that section of Wauchier's work which is attributed
to him, a section consisting of short, picturesque, and mutually
independent tales, which formed part of a popular collection.
It is misleading to speak as if Wauchier refers to him as
general source for his *Perceval* continuation; the references
are clearly marked and refer to *Gawain* tales. Apart from the
fact that Wauchier's reference does not stand alone we have
independent evidence of the actual existence of such a group
of tales, in our surviving *Gawain* poems, certain of which,
such as *Kay and the Spit,* and *Golagros and Gawayne* are
versions of the stories given by Wauchier, while the author
of the *Elucidation* was also familiar with the same collection.
If evidence for the identity of Bleheris is incomplete, that
for his existence appears to be incontrovertible. Would it not
be more honest if such a would-be critic as the writer referred
to said, 'I do not choose to believe in the existence of Bleheris,
because it runs counter to my pre-conceived theory of the
evolution of the literature'? We should then know where
we are. Such a parallel as that cited above has no value
for those familiar with the literature but may easily mislead
the general reader. I would also draw attention to the fact
noted in the text—the extreme improbability of Wauchier,
a continental writer, *inventing* an insular and Welsh source.
This is a point critics carefully evade.

late, the national legends. But we are dealing with variants of a proper name, and that of distinctly insular, and Welsh origin.[10]

The original form, Bledri, was by no means uncommon in Wales: from that point of view there might well have been four or five, or even more, of that name, but that each and all of these should have possessed the same qualifications, should have been equally well versed in popular traditions, equally dowered with the gift of story-telling, on equally friendly terms with the Norman invaders, and equally possessed of such a knowledge of the French language as should permit them to tell their stories in that tongue, is, I submit, highly improbable. This latter point, *i.e.*, the knowledge of French, seems to me to be of crucial importance. Given the relations between conqueror and conquered, and the *intransigeant* character of Welsh patriotism, the men who were on sufficiently friendly terms with the invaders to be willing to relate the national legends, with an assurance of finding a sympathetic hearing, must have been few and far between. I do not think the importance of this point has been sufficiently grasped by the critics.

The problem then is to find a Welshman who, living at the end of the eleventh and commencement of the twelfth centuries, was well versed in the legendary lore of Britain; was of sufficiently good social status to be well received at court; possessed a good knowledge of the French tongue; and can be shown to have been on friendly terms with the Norman nobles.

Mr Edward Owen, of the Cymmrodorion Soci-

---

[10] Cf. *Bledhericus de Cornouailles*, note contributed by M. Ferd. Lot, to *Romania*, Vol. xxvIII. p. 336. M. Lot remarks that he has not met with the name in Armorica; it thus appears to be insular.

ety, has suggested that a certain Welsh noble, Bledri ap Cadivor, fulfils, in a large measure, the conditions required. Some years ago I published in the *Revue Celtique* a letter in which Mr Owen summarized the evidence at his disposal. As the review in question may not be easily accessible to some of my readers I will recapitulate the principal points.[11]

The father of Bledri, Cadivor, was a great personage in West Wales, and is looked upon as the ancestor of the most important families in the ancient Dyfed, a division now represented by Pembrokeshire, and the Western portion of Carmarthen. (We may note here that the traditional tomb of Gawain is at Ross in Pembrokeshire, and that there is reason to believe that the *Perceval* story, in its earliest form, was connected with that locality.)

Cadivor had three sons, of whom Bledri was the eldest; thus, at his father's death, he would be head of this ancient and distinguished family. At the division of the paternal estates Bledri inherited, as his share, lands ranging along the right bank of the lower Towey, and the coast of South Pembrokeshire, extending as far as Manorbeer, the birthplace of Giraldus Cambrensis. (This is again a geographical indication which should be borne in mind.) Cadivor himself appears to have been on friendly terms with the Normans; he is said to have entertained William the Conqueror on his visit to St David's in 1080, while every reference we have to Bledri shows him in close connection with the invaders.

Thus, in 1113 the *Brut-y-Tywysogion* mentions his name as ally of the Norman knights in their struggle to maintain their ground in, and around, Carmarthen. In 1125 we find his name as donor of lands to the Augustinian Church of St John the Evangelist,

---

[11] Cf. *Revue Celtique*, 1911, *A note on the identification of Bleheris.*

and St Theuloc of Carmarthen, newly founded by
Henry I. Here his name appears with the significant
title *Latinarius* (The Interpreter), a qualification repeated in subsequent charters of the same collection.
In one of these we find Griffith, the son of Bledri,
confirming his father's gift. Professor Lloyd, in an
article in *Archaeologia Cambrensis*, July 1907, has
examined these charters, and considers the grant to
have been made between 1129 and 1134, the charter
itself being of the reign of Henry I, 1101-1135.[12]

In the Pipe Roll of Henry I, 1131, Bledri's name is
entered as debtor for a fine incurred by the killing
of a Fleming by his men; while a highly significant
entry records the fine of 7 marks imposed upon a
certain Bleddyn of Mabedrud and his brothers for
outraging Bledri's daughter. When we take into consideration the rank of Bledri, this insult to his family
by a fellow Welshman would seem to indicate that
his relations with his compatriots were not of a specially friendly character.

Mr Owen also points out that that portion of the
Brut-y-Tywysogion which covers the years 1101-1120
(especially the events of the year 1113, where we
find Bledri, and other friendly Welsh nobles, holding
the castle of Carmarthen for the Normans against the
Welsh), is related at an altogether disproportionate
length, and displays a strong bias in favour of the
invaders. The year just referred to, for instance,
occupies more than twice the space assigned to
any other year. Mr Owen suggests that here Bledri
himself may well have been the chronicler; a
hypothesis which, if he really be the author we are
seeking, is quite admissible.

So far as indications of date are concerned, Bledri
probably lived between the years 1070-1150. His

[12] Ed. Rhys-Evans, Vol. ii. p. 297; cf. also *Revue Celtique*.

father Cadivor died in 1089, and his lands were divided between his sons of whom Bledri, as we have seen, was the eldest. Thus they cannot have been children at that date; Bledri, at least, would have been born before 1080. From the evidence of the Pipe Roll we know that he was living in 1131. The charter signed by his son, confirmatory of his grant, must have been subsequent to 1148, as it was executed during the Episcopate of David, Bishop of St David's 1148–1176. Thus the period of 80 years suggested above (1070–1150) may be taken as covering the extreme limit to be assigned to his life, and activity.

The passage in which Giraldus Cambrensis refers to "Bledri, that famous story-teller 'who' lived shortly before our time," was written about 1194; thus it might well refer to a man who had died some 40 or 50 years previously. As we have noted above, Giraldus was born upon ground forming a part of Bledri's ancestral heritage, and thus might well be familiar with his fame.

The evidence is of course incomplete, but it does provide us with a personality fulfilling the main conditions of a complex problem. Thus, we have a man of the required name, and nationality; living at an appropriate date; of the requisite social position; on excellent terms with the French nobles, and so well acquainted with their language as to sign himself officially 'The Interpreter.' We have no direct evidence of his literary skill, or knowledge of the traditional history of his country, but a man of his birth could scarcely have failed to possess the latter, while certain peculiarities in that section of the national Chronicle which deals with the aid given by him to the Norman invaders would seem to indicate that Bledri himself may well have been responsible for the record. Again, we know him to have been closely connected with the locality from which came the writer who refers to the famous story-teller of the same name. I would submit that we have here quite sufficient evidence to warrant us in accepting Bledri ap Cadivor as, at least, the possible author of the romantic Grail tradition. In any case, so far, there is no other candidate in the field.[13]

Shortly after the publication of the second volume of my *Perceval* studies, I received a letter from Professor Singer, in which, after expressing his general acceptance of the theories there advanced, in especial of the suggested date and relation of the different versions, which he characterized as *"very successful and very much in accord with my own conception of the development of Old French literature,"* he proceeded to comment upon the probable character of the literary activity of Bleheris. His remarks are so interesting and suggestive that

---

[13] In the course of 1915–16 I received letters from Mr Rogers Rees, resident at Stepaside, Pembrokeshire, who informed me that he held definite proof of the connection of Bledri with both *Grail* and *Perceval* legends. The locality had been part of Bledri's estate, and the house in which he lived was built on the site of what had been Bledri's castle. Mr Rogers Rees maintained the existence of a living tradition connecting Bledri with the legends in question. At his request I sent him the list of the names of the brothers of Alain li Gros, as given in the 1516 edition of the *Perlesvaus*, a copy of which is in the Bibliothèque Nationale, and received in return a letter stating that the list must have been compiled by one familiar with the district. Unfortunately, for a year, from the autumn of 1916, I was debarred from work, and when, on resuming my studies, I wrote to my correspondent asking for the promised evidence I obtained no answer to my repeated appeal. On communicating with Mr Owen I found he had had precisely the same experience, and, for his part, was extremely sceptical as to there being any genuine foundation for our correspondent's assertions. While it is thus impossible to use the statements in question as elements in my argument, I think it right in the interests of scholarship to place them on record; they may afford a clue which some Welsh scholar may be able to follow up to a more satisfactory conclusion.

I venture to submit them for the consideration of my readers.

Professor Singer points out that in Eilhart von Oberge's *Tristan* we find the name in the form of *Pleherin* attached to a knight of *Mark's* court. The same name in a slightly varied form, *Pfelerin*, occurs in the *Tristan* of Heinrich von Freiberg; both poems, Professor Singer considers, are derived from a French original. Under a compound form, *Blihos*, (or *Blio*)-*Bliheris*, he appears, in the *Gawain-Grail* compilation, as a knight at *Arthur's* court. Now *Bréri-Blihis-Bleheris* is referred to as authority alike in the *Tristan*, *Grail* and *Gawain* tradition, and Professor Singer makes the interesting suggestion that these references are originally due to Bleheris himself, who not only told the stories in the third person (a common device at that period, *v*. Chrétien's *Erec*, and Gerbert's continuation of the *Perceval*), but also introduced himself as eye-witness of, and actor, in a subordinate *rôle*, in, the incidents he recorded. Thus in the *Tristan* he is a knight of Mark's, in the *Elucidation* and the *Gawain* stories a knight of Arthur's, court. Professor Singer instances the case of Dares in the *De exidio Trojae*, and Bishop Pilgrim of Passau in the lost *Nibelungias* of his secretary Konrad, as illustrations of the theory.

If this be the case such a statement as that which we find in Wauchier, regarding Bleheris's birth and origin, would have emanated from Bleheris himself, and simply been taken over by the later writer from his source; he incorporated the whole tale of the shield as it stood, a quite natural and normal proceeding.[14] Again, this suggestion would do away with the necessity for postulating a certain lapse

[14] Had Wauchier really desired to *invent* an authority, in view of his date, and connection with the house of Flanders, he had a famous name at hand—that of Chrétien de Troyes.

of time before the story-teller Bleheris could be
converted into an Arthurian knight—the two *"rôles,
author and actor,"* as Professor Singer expresses it,
are coincident in date. I would also suggest that
the double form, *Blihos-Bliheris,* would have been
adopted by the author himself, to indicate the
identity of the two, Blihis, and Bleheris. It is worthy
of note that, when dealing directly with the Grail,
he assumes the title of *Master,* which would seem
to indicate that here he claimed to speak with
special authority.

I sent the letter in question to the late Mr Alfred
Nutt, who was forcibly struck with the possibilities
involved in the suggestion, the full application of
which he thought the writer had not grasped.
I quote the following passages from the long letter
I received from him in return.

"Briefly put we presuppose the existence of a set
of semi-dramatic, semi-narrative, poems, in which
a Bledri figures as an active, and at the same time
a recording, personage. Now that such a body of
literature *may* have existed we are entitled to
assume from the fact that two such have survived,
one from Wales, in the Llywarch Hen cycle, the
other from Ireland, in the Finn Saga. In both cases,
the fact that the descriptive poems are put in the
mouth, in Wales of Llywarch, in Ireland largely of
Oisin, led to the ascription at an early date of the
whole literature to Llywarch and Oisin. It is therefore conceivable that a Welsh 'littérateur,' familiar as
he must have been with the Llywarch, and as he
quite possibly was with the Oisin, instance, should
cast his version of the Arthurian stories in a similar
form, and that the facts noted by you and Singer
may be thus explained."

Now that both Professor Singer (who has an
exceptionally wide knowledge of Medieval litera-

ture), and the late Mr Alfred Nutt, knew what they were talking about, does not need to be emphasized, and the fact that two such competent authorities should agree upon a possible solution of a puzzling literary problem, makes that solution worthy of careful consideration; it would certainly have the merit of simplifying the question and deserves to be placed upon record.

But while it would of course be far more satisfactory could one definitely place, and label, the man to whom we owe the original conception which gave birth and impetus to this immortal body of literature, yet the precise identity of the author of the earliest Grail romance is of the accident, rather than the essence, of our problem. Whether Bleheris the Welshman be, or be not, identical with Bledri ap Cadivor, Interpreter, and friend of the Norman nobles, the general hypothesis remains unaffected and may be thus summarized—

The Grail story is not *du fond en comble* the product of imagination, literary or popular. At its root lies the record, more or less distorted, of an ancient Ritual, having for its ultimate object the initiation into the secret of the sources of Life, physical and spiritual. This ritual, in its lower, exoteric, form, as affecting the processes of Nature, and physical life, survives to-day, and can be traced all over the world, in Folk ceremonies, which, however widely separated the countries in which they are found, show a surprising identity of detail and intention. In its esoteric 'Mystery' form it was freely utilized for the imparting of high spiritual teaching concerning the relation of Man to the Divine Source of his being, and the possibility of a sensible union between Man, and God. The recognition of the cosmic activities of the Logos appears to have been a characteristic feature of this teaching, and when Christianity came upon the scene it did not hesitate to utilize the already existing medium of instruction, but boldy identified the Deity of Vegetation, regarded as Life Principle, with the God of the Christian Faith. Thus, to certain of the early Christians, Attis was but an earlier manifestation of the Logos, Whom they held identical with Christ. The evidence of the Naassene document places this beyond any shadow of doubt, and is of inestimable value as establishing a link between pre-Christian, and Christian, Mystery tradition.

This curious synthetic belief, united as it was with the highly popular cult of Mithra, travelled with the foreign legionaries, adherents of that cult, to the furthest bounds of the Roman Empire and when the struggle between Mithraism and Christianity ended in the definite triumph of the latter, by virtue of that dual synthetic nature, the higher ritual still survived, and was celebrated in sites removed from the centres of population—in caves, and mountain fastnesses; in islands, and on desolate sea-coasts.

The earliest version of the Grail story, represented by our Bleheris form, relates the visit of a wandering knight to one of these hidden temples; his successful passing of the test into the lower grade of Life initiation, his failure to attain to the highest degree. It matters little whether it were the record of an actual, or of a possible, experience; the casting into romantic form of an event which the storyteller knew to have happened, had, perchance, actually witnessed; or the objective recital of what he knew *might* have occurred; the essential fact is that the *mise-en-scène* of the story, the nomenclature, the march of incident, the character of the tests, correspond to what we know from independent sources of the details of this Nature Ritual. The Grail Quest was actually possible then, it is actually possible to-day, for the indication of two of our romances as to the final location of the Grail is not imagination, but the record of actual fact.

As first told the story preserved its primal character of a composite between Christianity and the Nature Ritual, as witnessed by the ceremony over the bier of the Dead Knight, the procession with Cross and incense, and the solemn Vespers for the Dead. This, I suspect, correctly represents the final stage of the process by which Attis-Adonis was identified with Christ. Thus, in its first form the story was the product of conscious intention.

But when the tale was once fairly launched as a romantic tale, and came into the hands of those unfamiliar with its Ritual origin (though the fact that it had such an origin was probably well understood), the influence of the period came into play. The Crusades, and the consequent traffic in relics, especially in relics of the Passion, caused the identification of the sex Symbols, Lance and Cup, with the Weapon of the Crucifixion, and the Cup of the Last Supper; but the Christianization was merely external, the tale, as a whole, retaining its pre-Christian character.

The conversion into a definitely Christian romance seems to have been due to two causes. First, the rivalry between the two great monastic houses of Glastonbury and Fescamp, the latter of which was already in possession of a genuine *Saint-Sang* relic, and fully developed tradition. There is reason to suppose that the initial combination of the Grail and *Saint-Sang* traditions took place at Fescamp, and was the work of some member of the minstrel Guild attached to that Abbey. But the Grail tradition was originally British; Glastonbury was from time immemorial a British sanctuary; it was the reputed burial place of Arthur, of whose court the Grail Quest was the crowning adventure; the story must be identified with British soil. Consequently a version was composed, now represented by our *Perlesvaus* text, in which the union of Nicodemus of Fescamp, and Joseph of Glastonbury, fame, as ancestors of the Grail hero, offers a significant hint of the *provenance* of the version.

Secondly, a no less important element in the process was due to the conscious action of Robert de Borron, who well understood the character of his material, and radically remodelled the whole on the basis of the triple Mystery tradition translated into terms of high Christian Mysticism. A notable feature of Borron's version is his utilization of the tradition of the final Messianic Feast, in combination with his Eucharistic symbolism, a combination thoroughly familiar to early Christian Mystics.

Once started on a definitely romantic career, the Grail story rapidly became a complex of originally divergent themes, the most important stage in its development being the incorporation of the popular tale of the Widow's Son, brought up in the wilderness, and launched into the world in a condition of absolute ignorance of men, and manners. The *Perceval* story is a charming story, but it has originally nothing whatever to do with the Grail. The original tale, now best represented by our English *Syr Percyvelle of Galles*, has no trace of Mystery element; it is Folk-lore, pure and simple. I believe the connection with the Grail legend to be purely fortuitous, and due to the fact that the hero of the Folk-tale was known as 'The Widow's Son,' which he actually was, while this title represented in Mystery terminology a certain grade of

Initiation, and as such is preserved to-day in Masonic ritual.[15]

Finally the rising tide of dogmatic Medievalism, with its crassly materialistic view of the Eucharist; its insistence on the saving grace of asceticism and celibacy; and its scarcely veiled contempt for women, overwhelmed the original conception. Certain of the features of the ancient ritual indeed survive, but they are factors of confusion, rather than clues to enlightenment. Thus, while the Grail still retains its character of a Feeding Vessel, comes and goes without visible agency, and supplies each knight with 'such food and drink as he best loved in the world,' it is none the less the Chalice of the Sacred Blood, and critics are sorely put to it to harmonize these conflicting aspects. In the same way Galahad's grandfather still bears the title of the Rich Fisher, and there are confused references to a Land laid Waste as the result of a Dolorous Stroke.

But while the terminology lingers on to our perplexity the characters involved lie outside the march of the story; practically no trace of the old Nature Ritual survives in the final *Queste* form. The remodelling is so radical that it seems most reasonable to conclude that it was purposeful, that the original author of the *Queste* had a very clear idea of the real nature of the Grail, and was bent upon a complete restatement in terms of current orthodoxy. I advisedly use this term, as I see no trace in the *Queste* of a genuine Mystic conception, such

[15] Cf. *Legend of Sir Perceval*, Vol. II. p. 307 and note. I have recently received Dr Brugger's review of Mr R. H. Griffith's study of the English poem, and am glad to see that the critic accepts the independence of this version. If scholars can see their way to accept as *faits acquis* the mutual independence of the *Grail*, and *Perceval* themes, we shall, at last, have a solid basis for future criticism.

as that of Borron. So far as criticism of the literature is concerned I adhere to my previously expressed opinion that the *Queste* should be treated rather as a *Lancelot* than as a *Grail* romance. It is of real importance in the evolution of the Arthurian romantic cycle; as a factor in determining the true character and origins of the Grail legend it is worse than useless; what remains of the original features is so fragmentary, and so distorted, that any attempt to use the version as basis for argument, or comparison, can only introduce a further element of confusion into an already more than sufficiently involved problem.

I am also still of opinion that the table of descent given on p. 283 of Volume II. of my *Perceval* studies, represents the most probable evolution of the literature; at the same time, in the light of further research, I should feel inclined to add the Grail section of *Sone de Nansai* as deriving from the same source which gave us Kiot's poem, and the *Perlesvaus*.[16] As evidence for a French original combining important features of these two versions, and at the same time retaining unmistakably archaic elements which have disappeared from both, I hold this section of the poem to be of extreme value for the criticism of the cycle.

While there are still missing links in the chain of descent, versions to be reconstructed, writers to be identified, I believe that in its *ensemble* the theory set forth in these pages will be found to be the only one which will satisfactorily meet all the conditions of the problem; which will cover the whole ground of investigation, omitting no element, evading no difficulty; which will harmonize apparently hopeless contradictions, explain apparently

---

[16] Cf. my Notes, *Romania*, Vol. XLIII. pp. 403 *et seq.*

meaningless terminology, and thus provide a secure foundation for the criticism of a body of literature as important as it is fascinating.

The study and the criticism of the Grail literature will possess an even deeper interest, a more absorbing fascination, when it is definitely recognized that we possess in that literature a unique example of the restatement of an ancient and august Ritual in terms of imperishable Romance.

Index

ANCHOR BOOKS

LITERARY ESSAYS AND CRITICISM

10Ab

ANCHOR BOOKS

POETRY

THE AENEID OF VIRGIL—C. Day Lewis, trans., A20

AMERICAN POETRY AND POETICS: Poems and Critical Documents from the Puritans to Robert Frost—Daniel G. Hoffman, ed., A304

THE ANCHOR ANTHOLOGY OF SEVENTEENTH-CENTURY VERSE, Volume 1—Louis L. Martz, ed., ACO13a

THE ANCHOR ANTHOLOGY OF SEVENTEENTH-CENTURY VERSE, Volume 2—Richard S. Sylvester, ACO13b

AN ANTHOLOGY OF FRENCH POETRY from Nerval to Valery, in English Translation with French Originals—Angel Flores, ed., A134

AN ANTHOLOGY OF SPANISH POETRY from Garcilasco to Garcia Lorca, in English Translation with Spanish Originals—Angel Flores, ed., A268

ANTIWORLDS AND "THE FIFTH ACE"—Andrei Voznesensky; Patricia Blake, and Max Hayward, eds., a bilingual edition, A595

BRATSK STATION AND OTHER NEW POEMS—Yevgeny Yevtushenko; Tina Tupikina-Glaessner, Geoffrey Dutton, and Igor Nezhakoff-Koriakin, trans., intro. by Rosh Ireland, A558

THE CANTERBURY TALES OF GEOFFREY CHAUCER—Daniel Cook, ed., A265

COLLECTED POEMS—Robert Graves, A517

THE COMPLETE POETRY OF JOHN MILTON—John T. Shawcross, ed., revised edition, ACO15

THE COMPLETE POEMS AND SELECTED LETTERS AND PROSE OF HART CRANE—Brom Weber, ed., A537

THE COMPLETE POETRY OF JOHN DONNE—John T. Shawcross, ed., ACO11

THE COMPLETE POETRY OF RICHARD CRASHAW—George Walton Williams, ed., ACO14

A CONTROVERSY OF POETS: An Anthology of Contemporary American Poetry—Paris Leary and Robert Kelly, eds., A439

ENGLISH RENAISSANCE POETRY: A Collection of Shorter Poems from Skelton to Jonson—John Williams, ed., A359

ENGLISH ROMANTIC POETRY, Volume I: Blake, Wordsworth, Coleridge and Others—Harold Bloom, ed., A347a

ENGLISH ROMANTIC POETRY, Volume II: Byron, Shelley, Keats and Others—Harold Bloom, ed., A347b

THE FAR FIELD—Theodore Roethke, AO20

FORM AND VALUE IN MODERN POETRY—R. P. Blackmur, A96

GOETHE'S FAUST—Walter Kaufmann, trans., bilingual edition, A328

IN PRAISE OF KRISHNA: Songs from the Bengali—Denise Levertov and Edward C. Dimock, Jr., trans.; Anju Chaudhuri, illus., A545

INSIDE OUTER SPACE: New Poems of the Space Age—Robert Vas Dias, ed., A738

13Ab